SAS® Macro Language Magic

Discovering Advanced Techniques

Robert Virgile

support.sas.com/bookstore

The correct bibliographic citation for this manual is as follows: Virgile, Robert. 2013. *SAS® Macro Language Magic: Discovering Advanced Techniques*. Cary, NC: SAS Institute Inc.

SAS® Macro Language Magic: Discovering Advanced Techniques

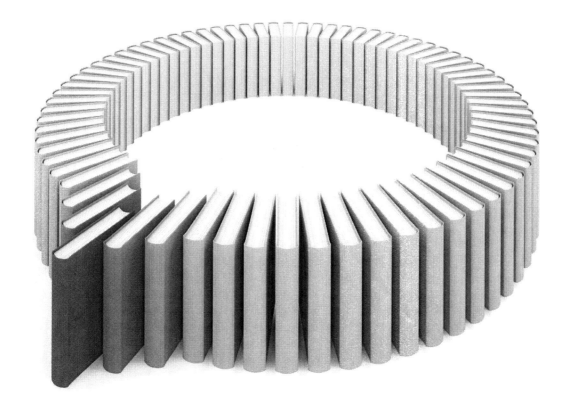

Gain Greater Insight into Your SAS® Software with SAS Books.

Discover all that you need on your journey to knowledge and empowerment.

support.sas.com/bookstore
for additional books and resources.

THE POWER TO KNOW®

Contents

About This Book

Purpose

This book is a roadmap to expert use of macro language. It reveals the secrets, explains the tricks, and covers the programming techniques. While syntax is occasionally necessary, the focus is on exploring, testing, and experimenting. Push the software to its limits to discover what works, what fails, and what the possibilities are.

This book dives deep into advanced concepts. Nobody is going to sit down and read it cover to cover. Approach the subject from a different angle. Plan on reading until you discover an astounding idea or technique. Would you like to:

- Create an output file, similar to the .log and .lst files, that automatically reflects the name of the program?
- Halt a program as soon as the first error occurs?
- Run a program using the version of all macros that was in place six months ago?

Once you find a technique that you like, work with your own macros for a while to fit that technique into the appropriate places. Reading starts you on the road toward magical macros. Practice ingrains the techniques, making them easy and natural.

Is This Book for You?

By its nature macro language is a subject for experienced SAS programmers. Macro language generates SAS code, and a programmer must be able to envision the SAS code needed to solve a programming problem in order to make effective use of macro language. If you need to review the syntax in more detail, SAS Press publishes good references:

- *SAS 9.4: Macro Language: Reference*
- *Carpenter's Guide to the SAS Macro Language, Second Edition*
- *SAS Macro Programming Made Easy, Second Edition*

This is the book that will take your skills to the next level.

Software Used to Develop This Book's Content

SAS 9.3 was used to create the examples in this book.

The SAS data sets and programs used in this book are available from the author page at http://support.sas.com/virgile.

Example Code and Data

Access the example SAS code and data for this book by linking to its author page at http://support.sas.com/virgile.

For an alphabetical listing of all books for which example code and data is available, see http://support.sas.com/bookcode. Select a title to display the book's example code.

If you are unable to access the code through the Web site, send e-mail to saspress@sas.com.

Additional Resources

SAS offers you a rich variety of resources to help build your SAS skills and explore and apply the full power of SAS software. Whether you are in a professional or academic setting, we have learning products that can help you maximize your investment in SAS.

Bookstore	http://support.sas.com/bookstore/
Training	http://support.sas.com/training/
Certification	http://support.sas.com/certify/
SAS Global Academic Program	http://support.sas.com/learn/ap/
SAS OnDemand	http://support.sas.com/learn/ondemand/
Knowledge Base	http://support.sas.com/resources/
Support	http://support.sas.com/techsup/
Training and Bookstore	http://support.sas.com/learn/
Community	http://support.sas.com/community/

Keep in Touch

We look forward to hearing from you. We invite questions, comments, and concerns. If you want to contact us about a specific book, please include the book title in your correspondence.

To Contact the Author through SAS Press

By e-mail: saspress@sas.com

Via the Web: http://support.sas.com/author_feedback

SAS Books

For a complete list of books available through SAS, visit http://support.sas.com/bookstore.

Phone: 1-800-727-3228

Fax: 1-919-677-8166

E-mail: sasbook@sas.com

SAS Book Report

Receive up-to-date information about all new SAS publications via e-mail by subscribing to the SAS Book Report monthly eNewsletter. Visit http://support.sas.com/sbr.

About The Author

Robert Virgile is an independent SAS trainer and consultant, with 30 years of experience developing and teaching SAS classes. He has published numerous papers and written problem-solving contests for the Northeast SAS Users Group (NESUG) and SAS Global Forum. Due to his wealth of SAS knowledge, Robert was barred from participating in the NESUG SAS Bowl.

Robert is also the author of *An Array of Challenges-Test Your SAS Skills* and *Efficiency: Improving the Performance of Your SAS Applications*.

Learn more about this author by visiting his author page where you can download a free chapter, access the example code and data for this book, read the latest reviews, get updates, and more:

http://support.sas.com/virgile

Acknowledgments

It took a village to write this book. The village started out small, as my wife Paula supported me by cheerfully allowing me the time and attention that it takes to write a book. But the village quickly expanded.

Writing and programming both build upon what others have done. Many programmers contributed ideas, shared code, or started the thought processes moving in a fruitful direction. Thanks go to Haikuo Bian, Art Carpenter, Craig Dickstein, Paul Dorfman, Ron Fehd, Judy Loren, Phil Mason, and Ian Whitlock. Other people deserve to be mentioned, but were difficult to track down. I utilized one idea from a SAS Communities post, and asked the author (Tom Abernathy) if he would like to be mentioned here. He responded that he had seen the idea in an earlier John King post. When I contacted John King, he also noted that he was not the original author.

SAS Publications staff were remarkable throughout. Julie Platt orchestrated SAS's efforts, and helped shepherd through my nit-picking contract requirements. The technical reviewers (Pat Garrett and Russ Tyndall) did a stellar job. Senior Editor John West survived the added burden of dealing with my frequent requests. Kathy Restivo edited and revised the copy to make it more readable. And Cindy Puryear designed the marketing plan beginning with the astounding book cover that you have already seen.

Finally, thanks also go out to the many end users who, through their unrelenting requests, forced me to develop some of these techniques. I hope you can build upon what you find here.

Part 1: Preparation

What makes a macro look like magic? How can a short macro enable an end user to generate sophisticated, accurate results? To write such macros, programming wizards apply their knowledge, boosted by creativity and years of experience. Of course, preparation begins with:

- Reading
- Taking courses
- Programming

But magical results require more preparation than that. Behind the scenes, these same programming wizards also:

- Strive to write simple programs.
- Keep up with advances in the software.
- Experiment to determine how the software really works.

They appreciate the relationship between the SAS language and macro language. The vast majority of macro applications generate SAS code. As a result, any steps that improve your SAS skills will broaden the range of SAS programs you can envision and increase the value of the macro language. These steps go hand in hand:

- Expand your knowledge of SAS software.
- Select a simpler, more appropriate SAS tool to accomplish a programming task.
- Write simpler, more powerful macros.

The first two chapters of this book illustrate these preparatory steps. Chapter 1, "SAS Language Preparation," focuses on the SAS language with a little bit of macro language mixed in. Chapter 2, "Shifting Gears: Macro Language," shifts the focus more heavily into the macro language.

Chapter 1: SAS Language Preparation

Macro language is useless unless you can visualize the SAS program that results. So we begin by examining the three learning steps and how they apply using the SAS language. This chapter emphasizes simplicity, keeping current, and experimentation.

1.1 Keep It Simple

Perhaps you have never seen:

- A one-page macro to perform character-to-numeric conversion (instead of using the INPUT function)
- A multi-page program to present three-dimensional tables in two dimensions (instead of using the LIST option within PROC FREQ).

Unfortunately, such complex programs exist. Make a point of simplifying your programs so that they won't need to be added to this list.

This first simplification uses statements that might appear in a DATA step. The original version is overly complex:

```
data last_one;
   set municipalities;
   by state county town;
   if last.state or last.county or last.town;
run;
```

When LAST.STATE or LAST.COUNTY is true, the condition LAST.TOWN must also be true. Therefore, a somewhat simpler program will generate the exact same result:

```
data last_one;
    set municipalities;
    by state county town;
    if last.town;
run;
```

Without macro language, the difference is trivial. But suppose a macro parameter holds the list of BY variables:

```
by_varlist=state county town,
```

If macro language has to generate one program versus the other, the workload becomes very different. We will revisit this scenario in Chapter 2.

Common programming tasks abound with opportunities for simplification. Compare these two ways to conclude a DATA step:

```
if eof then do;                 if eof;
    average = total / n;        average = total / n;
    output;                     run;
end;
run;
```

The shorter ending generates the same result. A more complete application calculates means within BY groups. A few different styles exist, including this common one:

```
data totals;
    set dairy;
    by cow;
    if first.cow then do;
       tot_milk=0;
       milkings = 0;
    end;
    tot_milk + (2*pints + 4*quarts);
    milkings + 1;
    if last.cow;
    average_milking = tot_milk / milkings;
run;
```

However, a variation in style generates a shorter program:

```
data totals;
    set dairy;
    by cow;
    tot_milk + (2*pints + 4*quarts);
```

```
      milkings + 1;
      if last.cow;
      average_milking = tot_milk / milkings;
      output;
      tot_milk=0;
      milkings=0;
   run;
```

The revised version might look a little awkward at first. But besides being a line shorter, it removes a level of indentation and actually runs slightly faster. Notice how the first version checks every observation for both FIRST.COW and LAST.COW, but the revised version checks only for LAST.COW.

Consider this all-too-common case of overly complex code.

1.1.1 Programming Challenge #1

Simplify the program, eliminating any unnecessary steps:

```
proc sort data=midwest;
   by state;
run;

data midwest;
   set midwest;
   counter=1;
run;

proc means data=midwest sum maxdec=0;
   class state;
   var counter;
   title 'Number of Observations for Each Midwest State';
run;
```

1.1.2 Solution

Certainly, the PROC SORT is unnecessary. The CLASS statement works with unsorted data. But there is more to eliminate. If you are having trouble locating the extra complexities, focus on the title before reading any further.

The key is figuring out what the program is trying to achieve. Because it counts the number of observations for each STATE, this replacement might come to mind:

```
proc freq data=midwest;
   tables state;
   title 'Number of Observations for Each Midwest State';
run;
```

A number of themes are emerging here. Choose simple, direct SAS tools. The simpler the SAS code, the simpler the macro version will be. Increase your knowledge of SAS to expand the variety of tools available for tackling a given programming problem. The more tools that you have at your disposal, the better your chances of constructing a simpler looking program. And the simpler the SAS code, the easier it is to write and to maintain the macro version.

Along those lines, here are a few suggested topics for independent self-study. Learn how to:

- Use the CNTLIN= option on PROC FORMAT to create a format from a SAS data set.
- Use the Output Delivery System (ODS) to capture procedure output as a SAS data set.
- Extract information from dictionary tables.

These topics will serve you well, even if you never venture into the world of the macro language.

1.2 Keep Up with the Software

Keep up with advances in the software. Even though SAS is continually advancing the software, many of the advances are not key breakthroughs. Rather, they fall into the category of nice (rather than essential) tools that make programming easier.

Begin with a simple example. The LENGTH function has a special feature:

```
len_name = length(name);
```

When the incoming string is blank, the function returns a 1 instead of a 0. This code would bypass that special feature:

```
if (name > ' ') then len_name = length(name);
else len_name=0;
```

However, a newer function eliminates the need for this bypass operation:

```
len_name = lengthn(name);
```

Unaware of this new feature, a macro programmer might code:

```
if (&varname > ' ') then len_&varname = length(&varname);
else len_&varname = 0;
```

But the macro version should be simpler:

```
len_&varname = lengthn(&varname);
```

Of course the macro version assumes that incoming variable names are no longer than 28 characters, so that LEN_&VARNAME contains a maximum of 32 characters.

Let's move on to another outdated example. Renaming a list of variables used to be tedious:

```
data new;
    set old (rename=(v1=var1 v2=var2 v3=var3
                     v4=var4 v5=var5 v6=var6
                     v7=var7 v8=var8 v9=var9
                     v10=var10));
    * more processing;
run;
```

If a macro were to perform the renaming, the DATA step might look like this:

```
data new;
    set old (rename=(%RENAMING(prefix_in=v, prefix_out=var,
                              first_num=1, last_num=10)));
    * more processing;
run;
```

The macro would be especially handy if there were large numbers of variables to rename or many sets of variables to rename. Here is one form that such a macro might take:

```
%macro renaming (prefix_in=, prefix_out=,
                 first_num=1, last_num=);
    %local i;
    %do i=&first_num %to &last_num;
        &prefix_in.&i=&prefix_out.&i
    %end;
%mend renaming;
```

In fact, there was a time when this level of complexity was necessary. But advances in the software have made it obsolete. Now the software can easily rename a list of variables:

```
data new;
    set old (rename=(v1-v10=var1-var10));
    * more processing;
run;
```

In the next example, the objective is to get rid of variable labels. This step might be needed in PROC MEANS, where the output prints the variable label as well as the variable name. If the labels are wide, the report might no longer fit each variable's information on a single line. The output gets split into sections instead. A simple way to condense the report is to wipe out the variable labels:

```
label var1=' '
      var2=' '
      var3=' '
```

```
var4=' '
    ...
varN=' ';
```

Most shorter approaches generate an error message, including:

```
label _all_=' ';
```

A macro could capture the names of all numeric variables in the data set and generate a LABEL statement for each. But a simple feature makes such a macro unnecessary:

```
attrib _all_ label=' ';
```

Just knowing that the simple tool is available makes writing a macro unnecessary.

The next example selects the last word from a series of words. For example, begin with this variable:

```
list_of_words = 'state county town';
```

The DATA step must select the word TOWN as the last word in this list. Here is the DATA step code, using the old-fashioned approach:

```
i=0;
length word $ 32;
if (list_of_words > ' ') then do;
   do until (word=' ');
      i + 1;
      word = scan(list_of_words, i, ' ');
   end;
   word = scan(list_of_words, i-1, ' ');
end;
```

When the SCAN function reaches past the end of the incoming list, it returns a blank. By reaching past the end of the list, the program can then go back and retrieve the last word.

Occasionally, an objective requires such complex code. But in this case, clever programming can dramatically shorten the code from nine statements to two:

```
length word $ 32;
word = reverse(scan(reverse(list_of_words), 1, ' '));
```

Reverse the original string, select the first word, and then reverse the characters in that first word. But advances in the software can simplify the code even further:

```
length word $ 32;
word = scan(list_of_words, -1, ' ');
```

When the second parameter contains a negative number, the SCAN function reads the list from right to left, instead of from left to right. By keeping up with advances in the software, a tricky problem becomes easy.

Consider one final example that works with the COMPRESS function. The existing variable PHONE_NUM holds phone numbers. But they are not in a standard format. These versions (as well as others) might appear in the data:

```
(123) 456-7890
123 456 7890
123 456-7890
123-456-7890
[123] 4567890
```

In order to transform all phone numbers into an identical format, you might begin by removing non-numeric characters. By guessing well, you might eliminate all non-numeric characters:

```
phone_num = compress(phone_num, '-() []');
```

Of course, there are only 256 possible characters, so the last parameter might specify the full set of 246 non-numerics. However, even that solution might not be transferable across operating systems. A better solution would automate instead of guessing:

```
phone_num = compress(phone_num, compress(phone_num,'1234567890'));
```

The interior COMPRESS function identifies all non-numeric characters, and the exterior COMPRESS function removes them.

But SAS 9 makes this task easy to accomplish and easy to read:

```
phone_num = compress(phone_num, '0123456789', 'K');
```

The third parameter indicates that the function should keep, rather than remove, characters found in the second parameter. In fact, that third parameter is quite powerful and supports:

```
phone_num = compress(phone_num,, 'KD');
```

The third parameter uses K for "keep" and D for "digits". So the program doesn't even have to spell out the list of digits.

Keeping up with the software will often enable you to write simpler programs.

1.3 Experiment

Whether the subject is cooking, sports, or programming, book learning has limitations. Testing and experimenting enrich the learning process far beyond what reading can do. Expect dismal failures. Expect delightful surprises. Expect to learn by experimenting.

Today's experiment is called "How Low Can You Go?" Can you assign a value to a variable such that either of these comparisons would be true:

```
if numval < . then put 'Found a small numeric!';
if charval < ' ' then put 'Found a small character!';
```

Book learning helps with the numeric value. The software supports 27 special missing values:

```
._  .A .B … .Z
```

Surveys routinely utilize these values to differentiate among various reasons a respondent failed to answer a question. For example, a survey might assign these values for respondents' answers:

1 = strongly agree
2 = agree
3 = neither agree nor disagree
4 = disagree
5 = strongly disagree

It would be inconvenient to assign these values as well:

6 = refused to answer
7 = not applicable
8 = departed the survey early

In that case, subsequent analyses would have to deal with values of 6, 7, and 8 separately for each question. Instead, this scale might be easier:

.A = refused to answer
.B = not applicable
.C = departed the survey early

Now a PROC MEANS would automatically exclude all forms of missing values from its calculations.

Are any of these special missing values lower than a traditional missing value? It turns out that just one of them is lower: ._ is lowest. So these statements would generate a true comparison:

```
numval = ._;
if numval < . then put 'Found a small numeric!';
```

Experimentation would confirm the order of special missing values, but it takes reading to discover that they exist. On the other hand, test programs reveal that there are 32 character values smaller than a blank:

```
data _null_;
   charval =' ';
   put charval $hex2.;
run;
```

In an ASCII environment, the PUT statement writes 20. So the hex codes ranging from 00 through 1F would all be lower than a blank. You won't find these characters on a keyboard, but you certainly can assign them in a program:

```
data test;
   do i=32 to 0 by -1;   /* when i is 32, hex code 20 = blank */
      hexcode = put(i, hex2.);
      charval = input(hexcode, $hex2.);
      output;
   end;
run;

proc sort data=test;
   by charval;
run;

proc print data=test;
run;
```

The results show that the blank falls to the end of the sorted list, whether sorting is performed by CHARVAL or by HEXCODE. All 32 other values for CHARVAL are smaller than a blank. (In an EBCDIC environment there are actually 64 characters smaller than a blank.)

The "How Low Can You Go?" experiment may be over, but do we really understand the software any better than before? These results give some insight into user-defined formats that define the range:

```
low - high
```

For numeric formats, missing values fall outside the range. But for character formats, blanks must be part of this range because there are characters smaller than a blank.

These experiments are just the beginning. As you conduct your own experiments, you will expand your understanding and comfort with the inner workings of the software. That's where the magic begins.

Let's shift into the realm of the macro language.

Chapter 2: Shifting Gears: Macro Language

As the focus shifts from the SAS language to the macro language, similar principles apply. It pays to expand your knowledge, to experiment, and to keep up with the latest software features, all the while attempting to keep programs as simple as possible. For example, just as the SCAN function can read a list from right to left, the %SCAN function can as well. Revisit this macro parameter from the beginning of Chapter 1:

```
by_varlist = state county town,
```

Based on that parameter, a macro must generate this code (with the bold sections based on &BY_VARLIST):

```
proc sort data=municipalities;
   by state county town;
run;

data last_one;
   set municipalities;
   by state county town;
   if last.town;
run;
```

The text substitution is easy (in two places):

```
by &by_varlist;
```

But how does macro language locate the last word in the list to create:

```
if last.town;
```

In years past the %SCAN function had to read from left to right, using %str( ) to indicate that blanks are the only delimiters. The answer looked something like this:

```
%local i;
%let i = 0;
%do %until (%scan(&by_varlist, &i+1, %str( ))=);
    %let i = %eval(&i + 1);
%end;
if last.%scan(&by_varlist, &i, %str( ));
```

The %DO loop continues to increment &I, until the next word in the list is blank. The result: the final value of &I matches the number of words in the list. The last statement retrieves that word.

Starting in SAS 8, the %SCAN function can read from right to left, enabling a simpler approach. The first five lines of code vanish, leaving only:

```
if last.%scan(&by_varlist, -1, %str( ));
```

Expanding your arsenal of tools is important. But equally important is experimenting with existing tools. Explore their limits without worrying about failure. To illustrate, consider some simple assignment statements:

```
%let ten=10;
%let twenty=20;
```

What would happen if we tried to get the same result this way?

```
%let ten=%let twenty=20; 10;
```

It turns out this generates an error message. The software won't begin a second %LET statement in the middle of an executing %LET statement. But what if we attempt to hide the structure:

```
data _null_;
    call symput('test', '%let twenty=20; 10');
run;
%let ten=&test;
```

There is still an error (although the error message changes). What about hiding the interior %LET statement in a macro, like this:

```
%macro test;
    %let twenty=20; 10
%mend test;
%let ten=%test;
```

Well, this version works! Executing %TEST assigns 20 as the value for &TWENTY and then generates the text 10 used as the value for &TEN. Why should this version work while the others fail? Experiments shed some light on the reasons and begin by assigning values to these macro variables:

```
%global ten twenty thirty;
data _null_;
    call symput('test1', '%let twenty=20; 10');
    call symput('test2', '%let thirty=30; %let twenty=20; 10');
    call symput('test3', '%let thirty=%let twenty=20; 30; 10');
run;
```

Outside of a macro definition, all of these statements would generate an error:

```
%let ten=&test1;  →  %let ten=%let twenty=20; 10;

%let ten=&test2;  →  %let ten=%let thirty=30; %let twenty=20; 10;

%let ten=&test3;  →  %let ten=%let thirty=%let twenty=20; 30; 10;
```

In every case, macro language interprets the resulting statements as beginning a %LET statement inside a partially completed %LET statement. However, defining macros can erase some of the error conditions. Remember that &TEN, &TWENTY, and &THIRTY are already defined as global variables:

```
%macro retrieve_test1;
    %let ten=;
    %let twenty=;
    %let thirty=;

    %let ten=&test1;  →  %let ten=%let twenty=20; 10;
%mend retrieve_test1;

%retrieve_test1
%put &ten;         →  10
%put &twenty;      →  20
%put &thirty;      →
```

In this case, all the %LET statements execute without error.

Here's the next experiment:

```
%macro retrieve_test2
    %let ten=;
    %let twenty=;
    %let thirty=;

    %let ten=&test2;  →  %let ten=%let thirty=30; %let twenty=20; 10;
%mend retrieve_test2;
```

```
%retrieve_test2
%put &ten;              →    10
%put &twenty;           →    20
%put &thirty;           →    30
```

Once again, the error messages vanish. The macro has embedded multiple %LET statements inside a %LET statement.

Try one final test:

```
%macro retrieve_test3;
    %let ten=;
    %let twenty=;
    %let thirty=;
    %let ten=&test3;   →    %let ten=%let thirty=%let twenty=20; 30; 10;
%mend retrieve_test3;

%retrieve_test3      →    Error!
%put &ten;
%put &twenty;
%put &thirty;
```

Finally, an error message surfaces: `Open code recursion detected.`

Do these results make sense? Why should the final test generate an error when the first two do not? Any conclusion we arrive at is really a theory, an explanation that we concoct that is consistent with the results of our experiments. Here is one such explanation. Evidently, the process of compiling a macro has an impact: the semicolons that appear within the macro definition get interpreted as ending the statements that appear within the macro. For example, %retrieve_test1 contains this statement:

```
%let ten=&test1;
```

By compiling the macro, the software determines that the semicolon it can "see" is the one that ends the %LET statement. Later, executing the macro generates this statement:

```
%let ten=%let twenty=20; 10;
```

Still, the software "remembers" that the final semicolon on the line is the one that ends the first %LET statement. It "figures out" that the interior semicolon ends the interior %LET statement.

Executing the macro does not change that interpretation. So executing the macro can add entire %LET statements, each one having its own semicolon, without introducing an error condition. However, executing the macro still cannot add two %LET statements that are embedded within one another. So %RETRIEVE_TEST3 can generate this statement:

```
%let ten=&test3;
```

During the macro compilation process, the software still determines that the semicolon it can "see" ends the %LET statement. But a problem arises when macro execution generates this statement:

```
%let ten=%let thirty=%let twenty=20; 30; 10;
```

The software still "remembers" that the final semicolon on the line ends the first %LET statement. But the section of the statement in bold is all new, generated code:

```
%let thirty=%let twenty=20; 30;
```

As newly generated code, what should this statement mean? The possibilities are:

- Assign &TWENTY a value of "20" and &thirty a value of "30"
- Assign &THIRTY a value of "`%let twenty=20; 30`"

Rather than try to figure out what you meant (or perhaps for other technical reasons that are hidden inside the black box of macro language), the software generates an error. Overall, however, our experimentation has discovered cases where it is possible to embed multiple statements within a %LET statement. Chapter 6 contains an example that utilizes this discovery.

In essence, we now have a theory. As part of the macro compilation process, the software interprets the semicolons it can "see" as ending the statements it can "see". Can we isolate those conditions, and simplify our experiments, to support that theory? Here is just one supporting test:

```
data _null_;
   call symput ('semicolon', ';');
run;

%put &semicolon;            → null

%macro supporting_test;
   %put &semicolon;
%mend supporting_test;
%supporting_test           → ;
```

Twice, this program generates:

```
%put ;;
```

The first time, when the generated text appears in open code, the software interprets this as being two statements. The first semicolon ends the %PUT statement. So the %PUT statement writes nothing, and then a null statement appears. The second time, when the macro call generates the %PUT statement, the software interprets the entire generated code as a single statement. The macro compilation process has already determined that the semicolon it can "see" ends the %PUT statement. Therefore, executing the macro causes %PUT to write a semicolon. Chapter 7 contains another example utilizing this discovery. For now, though, consider that our theory might not be limited to semicolons. It might apply to parentheses as well, as in this statement:

```
%let b = %length (&a);
```

Would it be possible that this statement could produce different results, depending on whether it appears inside or outside a macro? Here is the macro that will test that theory:

```
%macro length_test;
    %let b1 = %length(&balanced);
    %let b2 = %length(&right_only);
%mend length_test;
```

The tests will run on two incoming strings:

```
%let balanced = (text)ing;
%let right_only = text)ing;
%let b1 = %length(&balanced);
%let b2 = %length(&right_only);
%put &b1;                → 9
%put &b2;                → 4)ing
%length_test
%put &b1;                → 9
%put &b2;                → 4)ing
```

Evidently, the rules that apply to semicolons don't apply to right-hand parentheses. In compiling the macro, the software doesn't determine that the right parenthesis it can "see" is the one that defines the characters that %LENGTH should measure.

Let's consider one more experiment. An interactive session can appear unresponsive for a number of reasons. Besides forgetting a final RUN statement, the cause might be:

- An embedded comment began with `/*` but was never ended.
- A macro definition is missing a %MEND statement.
- There are unmatched quotes (either single or double).

Under any of these circumstances, additional code can be submitted but will not run. The color-coded program editor can help identify some of these conditions. And it would be nicer still if the interactive

Run menu were to include an option to clear out all already submitted statements, allowing you to start over. Submitting this magical string might refresh a hung session:

```
*);*/;/*'*/ /*"*/; %MEND;run;quit;;;;;
```

But this is a lot to remember. Would it be possible to capture this code as a macro variable? A DATA step would certainly allow it:

```
call symput('fixit', '*);*/;/*''*/ /*"*/; %MEND;run;quit;;;;;');
```

However, this is not a viable approach to refreshing a hung session. Issuing this statement won't be sufficient:

```
&fixit
```

If the cause of the hang-up is unbalanced single quotes or an unfinished macro definition, the macro variable won't resolve. Remember, if all your experiments succeed, it's a sign that you are not experimenting enough!

Besides experimenting and expanding your list of tools, be creative with the ones that you have. Compare these two statements, for example:

```
%if &total < 0 %then %put WARNING;
%if &total < 0 %then %put WAR%str()NING;
```

Clearly, both statements generate the same result. However, the second statement is an improvement. Why? Because if you search the log for the word WARNING, you will always find it with the first statement. With the second, you only find a WARNING when the logic (&TOTAL < 0) has generated the word WARNING.

Even a simple comment statement can take on different formats. Compare these two approaches:

```
%* This is a comment that        %** This is a comment that ;
   spans two lines.;             %** spans two lines.        ;
```

The second approach has a distinct advantage. It allows text-searching tools to easily locate and/or extract all the comment lines within a program.

Even when using the simplest of tools, tinker. Ponder how they could be used. Understanding what they do is just the starting point.

As we move on to the next set of chapters, we will explore a variety of tools and concepts, both old and new. Experimentation and pushing the tools to the limit will abound throughout.

Part 2: Technique

The right set of tools makes any job easier, but knowing how to use them is equally important. Chapters 3 through 9 examine several macro language tools and concepts, but they de-emphasize syntax. Instead, these chapters push, prod, and experiment with the tools, generating insights into how they really work. Although many of the tools may appear familiar, these chapters expand the ways they can be applied. Expect to find:

- A macro variable that generates different text each time it gets resolved.
- A series of IF/THEN/ELSE statements generated by PROC SQL.
- User-created output files that automatically utilize the name of the program, just like .log and .lst files.

Along the way, this section presents some tough programming challenges, difficult enough to test even the best of programmers. Think about them and try to solve them, but don't worry about keeping score. The real prize is what you learn.

Chapter 3: CALL EXECUTE

The CALL EXECUTE statement toils in relative obscurity. Despite its power, and despite the fact that it has been available for many years, relatively few programmers are familiar with it. As a result, this section presents some of the basics as well as the intricacies.

3.1 Basic Rules

CALL EXECUTE is a DATA step statement that means: "Run this code." Here is an overly simple example:

```
data sales;
   call execute ('proc print data=sales; run;');
   amount=5;
run;
```

Even though CALL EXECUTE asks for a PROC PRINT to run, it is impossible to run a PROC PRINT in the middle of a DATA step. So SAS holds that code aside. PROC PRINT runs once the DATA step completes, just as if the program were:

```
data sales;
    amount=5;
run;
proc print data=sales;
run;
```

These basic rules govern code generated with CALL EXECUTE:

- The statements run as soon as possible.
- The statements can be data-driven. The expression inside parentheses can include reference to DATA step variables, not just quoted strings.
- A single DATA step can include multiple CALL EXECUTE statements. Any generated SAS code just stacks up, word by word, to run once the DATA step is over.
- Always include the RUN statement at the end of the DATA step.

While we'll add some more complex rules shortly, just these simple rules can produce magical results.

3.2 Achieving the Impossible

The first bit of magic revisits that "impossible" task of combining DATA and PROC steps:

```
data _null_;
    set sales end=nomore;
    total + amount;
    if nomore;
    if (total < 1000000) then do;
        proc means data=sales;
            class state;
            var amount;
            title "Sales by State";
        run;
    end;
    else do;
        proc means data=sales;
            class state year;
            var amount;
            title "Sales by State and Year";
        run;
    end;
run;
```

The intent is that the DATA step should calculate the total of all the AMOUNTs and use that to determine which version of PROC MEANS should run. Of course, there are numerous reasons why this code will fail. Mixing DATA and PROC steps generates errors, and the presence of three RUN statements will surely cause problems. But CALL EXECUTE easily overcomes these obstacles:

```
data _null_;
   set sales end=nomore;
   total + amount;
   if nomore;
   if (total < 1000000) then
   call execute('
      proc means data=sales;
         class state;
         var amount;
         title "Sales by State";
      run;
   ');
   else call execute('
      proc means data=sales;
         class state year;
         var amount;
         title "Sales by State and Year";
      run;
   ');
run;
```

The revised DATA step replaces DO groups with CALL EXECUTE statements. As planned, the DATA step adds up all the AMOUNTs and then uses CALL EXECUTE to determine which version of PROC MEANS executes once the DATA step is over. And the program is nearly identical to the failing version. This example illustrates one of the basic times CALL EXECUTE comes in handy: when the program must integrate DATA step variables into the subsequent PROC step.

Another impossible task: %IF %THEN statements cannot appear in open code. These statements are legal but only within a macro definition:

```
%if &city = Boston %then %do;
   proc means data=beantown;
      var pahk youh caah;
   run;
%end;
%else %if &city = New York %then %do;
   proc means data=big_apple;
      var a nominal egg;
   run;
%end;
```

The only purpose of adding %MACRO and %MEND statements in this program would be to permit the use of %IF %THEN statements. Could CALL EXECUTE help here? It eliminates the need to define a macro by substituting DATA step IF THEN statements for macro %IF %THEN statements:

```
data _null_;
    if "&city" = "Boston" then call execute('
        proc means data=beantown;
            var pahk youh caah;
        run;
    ');
    else if "&city" = "New York" then call execute('
        proc means data=big_apple;
            var a nominal egg;
        run;
    ');
run;
```

True, the results will be different if &CITY contains leading blanks. Correcting that is easy enough, however. Better programs will, as a rule, handle rare but foreseeable circumstances. Section 4.4 presents another workaround that gets results equivalent to using %IF %THEN without defining a macro.

3.3 Multiple CALL EXECUTEs

Multiple CALL EXECUTE statements can build a more sophisticated program. The incoming SAS data set named CUTOFFS illustrates this point. Assume that the observations are sorted as shown, from highest to lowest SAT_CUTOFF:

Obs	SAT_cutoff	Group_name
1	1200	Honor students
2	900	Regular track
3	300	Challenged

The DATA step must use CUTOFFS to construct the following program, extracting the data values in **bold**:

```
data student_groups;
    set all_students;
    length group $ 14;
    if score >= 1200 then group='Honor students';
    else if score >= 900 then group='Regular track';
    else if score >= 300 then group='Challenged';
run;
```

CALL EXECUTE does the job, using neither a macro nor any macro variables. (As usual, the spacing and indentation are for readability only and have no impact on the program's results.)

```
data _null_;
   set cutoffs end=lastone;
   if _n_=1 then call execute("data student_groups;
                                 set all_students;
                                 length group $ 14;");
   call execute("if score >= ");
   call execute(put(SAT_cutoff, best16.));
   call execute(" then group = '");
   call execute(group_name || "';");
   if lastone=0 then call execute("else ");
   else call execute("run;");
run;
```

The first CALL EXECUTE runs just once, generating the DATA, SET, and LENGTH statements. The next set of four CALL EXECUTE statements runs for each observation in CUTOFFS. They generate an IF THEN statement (without the word ELSE). The next-to-last CALL EXECUTE runs for each observation except the last one, adding ELSE before a subsequent IF THEN statement. The final CALL EXECUTE runs just once, adding a RUN statement.

Although beauty is in the eye of the beholder, it would have been possible to combine the set of four CALL EXECUTE statements into a single statement:

```
call execute("if score >= " || put(SAT_cutoff, best16.)
               || " then group = '" || group_name || "';");
```

This program illustrates a few features of a realistic application:

- Multiple CALL EXECUTE statements each generate separate sections of the program.
- The arguments to CALL EXECUTE contain complex expressions.
- Data values contribute to the generated SAS code.

3.4 Finally, the Intricacies

If those are the basics, what are the intricacies? One intricacy is that the software must have already interpreted the entire DATA step in order to run. So CALL EXECUTE cannot impact the current DATA step in any way. Neither of these statements would impact the running DATA step:

```
call execute ('pi=3.14;');
call execute ('options obs=10;');
```

Another intricacy involves the need for a RUN statement at the end of the DATA step. When a RUN statement ends the DATA step, it signals that the DATA step is complete and should run immediately. The software stops parsing and starts executing. But what would happen without a RUN statement?

```
data _null_;
   call execute ('proc print data=sales;');
```

```
        var state amount;
    run;
```

Should the software ignore the missing RUN statement and generate PROC PRINT before the VAR statement?

```
data _null_;
    call execute ('var state amount;');
proc print data=sales;
    run;
```

Should the software parse the complete PROC PRINT statement and then allow CALL EXECUTE to add the VAR statement?

```
data _null_;
    call execute ('data=sales;');
    proc print
    var state amount;
    run;
```

Should the software parse just the two words PROC and PRINT and allow CALL EXECUTE to complete the PROC statement? The real answer is: "Don't do it." CALL EXECUTE without a RUN statement is improper, unsupported syntax. It is even possible that the results would be inconsistent from one release of the software to the next.

The final complexity is that macro statements execute immediately, when generated by CALL EXECUTE. They do not stack up, waiting for the DATA step to finish. So let's revisit that idea that CALL EXECUTE cannot change the currently executing DATA step. By using SYMGET, it is actually possible to work around that limitation:

```
%let pet=CAT;
data test;
    call execute ('%let pet=DOG;');
    animal = symget('pet');
    put animal;  → DOG
run;
```

Before the DATA step executes, &PET is CAT. When CALL EXECUTE generates a %LET statement, that statement runs immediately, changing &PET to DOG. So ANIMAL receives the value of DOG. Just for the record, SYMGET defines ANIMAL as having a length of 200. When you are creating a DATA step variable using SYMGET, define that variable with a LENGTH statement first.

Notice how this feature of CALL EXECUTE, executing macro language statements immediately, can be useful. Normally, it is impossible for a DATA step to conditionally execute a %LET statement. Consider this DATA step as an example:

```
%let pet=CAT;
data _null_;
   if 5>4 then do;
      %let pet=DOG;
   end;
   if 5=4 then do;
      %let pet=RAT;
   end;
   animal = symget('pet');
   put animal;  → RAT
run;
```

Both %LET statements run during the compilation phase of the DATA step. Neither is part of the DATA step, and neither is affected by whether a DATA step IF THEN condition is true or false. Simply put, the DATA step cannot conditionally execute %LET statements, unless you utilize CALL EXECUTE:

```
%let pet=CAT;
data _null_;
   if 5>4 then do;
      call execute ('%let pet=DOG;');
   end;
   if 5=4 then do;
      call execute ('%let pet=RAT;');
   end;
   animal = symget('pet');
   put animal;  → DOG
run;
```

The DATA step can control whether CALL EXECUTE runs, and CALL EXECUTE can control the generation of a %LET statement. So with a little extra work, DATA steps can conditionally execute macro language statements such as %LET.

3.4.1 Programming Challenge #2

If all this seems easy, it's time to test yourself. Write a macro such that these programs generate different results:

```
%mymac data _null_;
   call execute('%mymac');
run;
```

Hint: The key feature that creates the difference between the programs is timing. Any macro language statements generated by CALL EXECUTE will run immediately. But any SAS language statements must stack up and wait until the current DATA step finishes.

3.4.2 Solution

A simple solution illustrates how timing makes the difference. Here is one possible definition of %MYMAC:

```
%macro mymac;
    %let color=blue;
    %put Color began as &color..;
    data _null_;
        call symput('color', 'red');
    run;
    %put Color ends up as &color..;
%mend mymac;
```

When the %MYMAC statement executes the macro, all its statements execute in order. The messages are:

```
Color began as blue.
Color ends up as red.
```

When CALL EXECUTE invokes the macro, however, the statements execute in a different order. All macro statements execute immediately:

```
%let color=blue;
%put Color began as &color..;
%put Color ends up as &color..;
```

But the DATA step statements (notably CALL SYMPUT) have to stack up and wait to execute. Therefore, the messages are:

```
Color began as blue.
Color ends up as blue.
```

3.5 Execute an Experiment

In both theory and practice, macro language statements generated by CALL EXECUTE run immediately. But there must be times when we would like to change that and have macro language statements wait until the current DATA step is over. Let's take an artificially simple example:

```
%let value = BEFORE;
data _null_;
    call execute('%let value = AFTER;');
    data_step_var = symget('value');
    put data_step_var;      →    AFTER
run;
%put Value is &value..;     →    Value is AFTER.
```

This program shows how the %LET statement generated by CALL EXECUTE runs immediately, without stacking up until the DATA step is over. SYMGET retrieves AFTER, the &VALUE assigned by the second %LET statement. Could we possibly change that? Could we find a way to force all statements generated by CALL EXECUTE, including macro language statements, to wait until the current DATA step finishes? In this program, the objective would be that SYMGET retrieves BEFORE. The %LET statement executes once the DATA step completes, so that the PUT statement writes BEFORE yet the %PUT statement writes AFTER.

Here are some failing experiments. Each one takes the same DATA step but replaces the CALL EXECUTE statement.

First, try to fool the macro processor by separating the % from the rest of the generated code:

```
call execute ('%' || 'let value = AFTER;');
```

Next, try to fool the macro processor into thinking a nonexistent macro is being called (%L):

```
call execute ('%L' || 'et value = AFTER;');
```

Next, try to bury the %LET statement, hiding it in a subsequent DATA step:

```
call execute
        ("data _null_; call execute('%let value = AFTER;'); run;");
```

None of these work. In every case, the %LET statement executes immediately, and DATA_STEP_VAR is assigned the value AFTER. However, combining the first and third attempts does work! The key steps:

- Split the %LET statement into pieces, so it is not easily recognizable.
- At the same time, bury the %LET statement inside a subsequently executing DATA step.

By itself, the CALL EXECUTE statement becomes:

```
call execute ("data _null_; call execute('%" ||
            "let value = AFTER;'); run;");
```

In context, the full program looks like this:

```
%let value = BEFORE;
data _null_;
   call execute ("data _null_; call execute('%" ||
            "let value = AFTER;'); run;");
   data_step_var = symget('value');
   put data_step_var;      →   BEFORE
run;
%put Value is &value..;    →   Value is AFTER.
```

Somehow, splitting the %LET statement hides it from the macro processor while the initial DATA step executes. The %LET statement doesn't execute until it is generated by the second DATA step.

These complexities are unnecessary, however. The software does contain the right tool for the job, a tool that temporarily hides from the macro processor the fact that a macro statement appears. By design, this variation successfully delays the execution of %LET:

```
%let value=BEFORE;
data _null_;
   call execute('%nrstr(%let value=AFTER;)');
   data_step_var = symget('value');
   put data_step_var;   →   BEFORE
run;
%put Value is &value..;   →   Value is AFTER.
```

The %NRSTR function is designed to mask macro references until the statement executes. That is enough to hide the %LET statement, delaying its execution until the DATA step is over. Chapter 7 will explore macro quoting functions in more detail.

3.6 The Final Intricacy: Macro Variable Resolution

Single quotes prevent macro variable resolution (as well as all other macro language activity). Therefore, the choice of single vs. double quotes makes a difference with combinations of CALL EXECUTE and CALL SYMPUT. Consider the following test:

```
%let value = BEFORE;
data _null_;
   call symput('value', 'AFTER');
   call execute("%put Double Quotes:  value is &VALUE..;");
   call execute('%put Single Quotes:  value is &VALUE..;');
run;
```

Both %PUT statements execute immediately. Double quotes permit resolution of &VALUE during the initial phase of the DATA step when statements are interpreted and checked for syntax errors. The first CALL EXECUTE generates:

```
Double Quotes:  value is BEFORE.
```

However, single quotes prevent resolution of &VALUE until later on, once the DATA step begins to execute. CALL EXECUTE still generates a %PUT statement, but that %PUT statement contains an unresolved &VALUE. As the DATA step executes, it replaces &VALUE with AFTER. When CALL EXECUTE generates its %PUT statement, &VALUE contains AFTER:

```
Single Quotes:  value is AFTER.
```

The same principle would apply if CALL EXECUTE were to generate SAS language statements, rather than macro language statements:

```
%let value = BEFORE;
data _null_;
   call symput('value', 'AFTER');
   call execute("proc print data=&VALUE.; run;");
   call execute('proc print data=&VALUE.; run;');
run;
```

The first CALL EXECUTE uses double quotes, so &VALUE resolves early:

```
proc print data=BEFORE; run;
```

But the second uses single quotes, so &VALUE resolves later:

```
proc print data=AFTER; run;
```

When CALL EXECUTE is the right tool for the job, it often simplifies a program dramatically. Based on your own experience, see if you can find an application that would benefit from using it.

Chapter 4: %SYSFUNC

The DATA step supports hundreds of functions. But the macro language contains a handful of functions, such as %SCAN and %SUBSTR. %SYSFUNC bridges the gap, permitting the macro language to utilize virtually all DATA step functions. (Technically, it can also utilize functions written using SAS/TOOLKIT software and PROC FCMP.)

Programmers apply functions in many ways, for many purposes. As a result, %SYSFUNC examples cover a broad range of applications. To the extent possible, this chapter focuses on typical, widely applicable examples.

4.1 Basic Examples

This first example lets macro language invoke the TODAY() function. %SYSFUNC's second parameter (*mmddyy10*) specifies the format for expressing the result:

```
%let currdate = %sysfunc(today(), mmddyy10);
```

If this code were to run on February 15, 2014, the result would be 02/15/2014. Even such a simple example has realistic applications. For example, consider this scenario:

- A program runs periodically, creating a permanent output data set each time it runs.

- All output data sets must be preserved, rather than reusing the same data set name each time.
- A convenient way to save the data sets would be to include the creation date as part of the data set name. Better yet, do it in a way where the alphabetized list of names happens to be in date order.

Half of one SAS statement achieves this result in its entirety:

```
data perm.dataset_%sysfunc(today(), yymmddn8);
```

The "n" in *yymmddn8* requests that there are "no" separators between the year, month, and day. So if this code were to run on February 15, 2014, it would generate:

```
data perm.dataset_20140215;
```

As long as the program never runs twice in the same day, each data set name will be unique. And by adding year/month/day as part of the name, the alphabetized list is also in date order.

%SYSFUNC can utilize nearly all DATA step functions. The most notable exception is that the PUT function is not supported. Instead, switch to either PUTN or PUTC. For example, this loop attempts to create three local macro variables:

```
%do i=001 %to 003;
    %local v&i;
%end;
```

While the intent is to create macro variables named v001, v002, and v003, this program fails. Instead, it creates v1, v2, and v3. The leading zeros are not part of the value of &I. To generate the desired names, %SYSFUNC comes to the rescue:

```
%do i=1 %to 3;
    %local v%sysfunc(putn(&i,z3));
%end;
```

Another common %SYSFUNC application is checking user-entered parameters. Chapter 11 contains many such examples. For now, here is a basic example:

```
%let rc = %sysfunc(exist(&dsn));
```

The EXIST function checks to see whether a SAS data set exists, returning either a 0 or a 1. So when a user supplies a data set name to a macro, the macro can detect whether that data set exists and take appropriate action.

Moving beyond these basic examples, the next section delves into one of the most widespread uses of %SYSFUNC.

4.2 Capturing the Program Name

This example applies to batch programs only:

```
%let program_path = %sysfunc(getoption(sysin));
```

GETOPTION retrieves information about the current program or session. By specifying SYSIN as the argument, the function retrieves the complete path to the current program. (This function cannot return a path when you are using SAS interactively.) Consider this simple application:

```
title "Program:  %sysfunc(getoption(sysin))";
```

Now the first title line will contain the complete path to the program that produced the output. And if the program gets moved or copied, the TITLE statement doesn't have to change. The next time the program runs, it will generate the path to the new program location. So with minimal effort, all your reports can automatically display the name of the source program.

Similar tools exist, including some that apply to the interactive use of SAS, but they are beyond the scope of this book. If this is an area of interest, consider:

- The view SASHELP.VEXTFL contains information about known external files, with the variable XPATH holding the path to each file. Any program brought into the enhanced program editor is automatically tracked in this view.

- In a Windows environment, the environmental variables SAS_EXECFILEPATH and SAS_EXECFILENAME can be retrieved using %SYSGET:

```
%put %sysget(SAS_EXECFILEPATH);
```

With a little imagination, applications can expand beyond the realm of TITLE statements. Suppose a long program produces a ton of output. Usually, the analyst is interested in just the final PROC PRINT, but the earlier output must be available in case there are any questions about the final report. Splitting the output in two would make life easier for the analyst: leave most of the output in the .lst file, but move the final PROC PRINT report to a separate file. In theory, the software supports this:

```
proc printto print="some_other_file" new;
run;
proc print data=final_results;
run;
```

But the harder part is linking the new output file with the original program. %SYSFUNC makes that task easy. These statements capture the full path to the program and then remove the last three letters (presumably removing the letters "sas" while leaving in place the "." at the end):

```
%let program_path = %sysfunc(getoption(sysin));
%let program_path = %substr(&program_path,1,%length(&program_path)-3);
```

Once the program has captured the program name and removed the letters "sas" from the end, redirect the final report to a matching file name:

```
proc printto print="&program_path.final_report" new;
run;
proc print data=final_results;
run;
```

The output includes the .lst file with all the earlier results, plus a new file holding the final PROC PRINT results. The name of that new file automatically matches the name of the program but with the extension .final_report. While Section 5.4 will embellish upon this technique, many objectives could benefit from creating output files that match the program name. Here are just a couple of examples:

- A program could use its results to generate the next program that should run, saving the next program in a file with a matching name. Creating a separate program gives the analyst an opportunity to inspect and approve the results of the first program before running the subsequent program.
- A program may process thousands of variables and save a list of variables that satisfy testing criteria. Saving that list in a separate file serves as documentation of the program results while making it easy to incorporate the list into subsequent programs.

4.3 Commas and Nested %SYSFUNCs

Even relatively simple applications can nest %SYSFUNCs. For example, consider an application that expresses an amount in the comma9 format and removes leading or trailing blanks. In a DATA step, the code might look like this:

```
without_blanks = compress( put(amount, comma11.) );
```

Of course, the DATA step could have issues with the preassigned length of WITHOUT_BLANKS, and it might add some trailing blanks. But the focus here is how to achieve a similar result using macro language. To illustrate the problem, temporarily split apart the nested functions. Here is one attempt that illustrates how %SYSFUNC must switch from PUT to PUTN:

```
%let without_blanks = %sysfunc(putn(&amount,comma11));

%let without_blanks = %sysfunc(compress(&without_blanks));
```

Presumably, the second statement resolves to something like:

```
%let without_blanks = %sysfunc(compress(    135,791));
```

Remember, the comma is a key symbol within the COMPRESS function, separating the string to compress and the characters to remove. So the macro language interprets this statement as saying: "Remove all instances of 1, 7, and 9 from the string 135." (The combination of %SYSFUNC and

COMPRESS automatically ignores the leading blanks in the first argument.) So the final value of &WITHOUT_BLANKS is 35. A single letter overcomes this problem:

```
%let without_blanks=%sysfunc(compress(%qsysfunc(putn(&amount,comma11))));
```

Switching to %QSYSFUNC quotes the results, turning the generated comma into text instead of a symbolic character. For more quoting examples, refer to Chapter 7.

Applications that insert the current date into the title could face a similar issue. Date formats are centered, and the WORDDATE18 format would contain a comma. That comma would cause a similar problem, forcing a switch from %SYSFUNC to %QSYSFUNC.

Finally, remember that there are other ways to remove leading and trailing blanks. An extra statement could replace COMPRESS:

```
%let without_blanks = %sysfunc(putn(&amount,comma11));
%let without_blanks = &without_blanks;
```

Or switch to STRIP instead of COMPRESS:

```
%let without_blanks = %sysfunc(strip(%sysfunc(putn(&amount,comma11))));
```

In the first example, the %LET statement ignores leading and trailing blanks to the right of the equal sign, so the second %LET statement automatically removes any leading or trailing blanks. In the second example, STRIP does not support a second parameter (at least not in current releases of the software). So the comma does not cause a problem.

Sometimes the presence of extra blanks is cosmetic, such as within a TITLE statement. But sometimes the extra blanks cause errors. Chapter 5 explores cases where removing blanks is essential.

4.4 Achieving the Impossible, Revisited

Section 3.2 showed how the CALL EXECUTE statement can circumvent the need to define a macro just to permit %IF %THEN statements. %SYSFUNC provides an alternative method, by invoking the IFN function, which requires three arguments (separated by commas):

- A true/false comparison
- A statement to perform when the condition is true
- A statement to perform when the condition is false

In a DATA step, this code could be replaced:

```
if amount > 10000 then type = 'Large';
else type = 'Small';
```

The IFN function requires one long statement:

```
type = ifn (amount > 10000, 'Large', 'Small');
```

To shift over to a macro language application, consider a simplified version of some code from Section 3.2:

```
%if &city = Boston %then %do;
    proc means data=beantown;
        var pahk youh caah;
    run;
%end;
%else %do;
    proc means data=big_apple;
        var a nominal egg;
    run;
%end;
```

The %IF %THEN statements cannot appear in open code. Although it would be clumsy, %SYSFUNC can circumvent the requirement of defining a macro:

```
%let which_one = %sysfunc( ifn( &city = Boston,
                    %str(proc means data=beantown;
                            var pahk youh caah;
                        run;),
                    %str(proc means data=big_apple;
                            var a nominal egg;
                        run;) ));
     &which_one
```

%SYSFUNC lets macro language invoke the IFN function, determining which set of statements get assigned to &WHICH_ONE. With no %IF %THEN statements, this approach works outside of a macro to generate the PROC PRINT that matches the value of &CITY.

4.5 Capturing Option Settings

Turning on all of these options generates an overwhelming amount of feedback:

```
options mprint mlogic symbolgen;
```

And yet, these options are useful temporarily when a section of a macro requires debugging. It is certainly easy to turn them off again:

```
options nomprint nomlogic nosymbolgen;
```

However, turning them off again may be the wrong action. Rather, a more complex set of steps might be better:

- Capture the current settings for these options.
- Turn all the options on, just before the troublesome section of macro code.
- Just after the troublesome section, set all the options back to their original settings, rather than turning them all off.

%SYSFUNC makes it easy to capture the current settings:

```
%let original_settings = %sysfunc(getoption(mprint))
                         %sysfunc(getoption(mlogic))
                         %sysfunc(getoption(symbolgen));
```

Turn on all options before the troublesome section and then reset them after:

```
options mprint mlogic symbolgen;
%* Troublesome section of code;
options &original_settings;
```

Depending on the macros in effect, it may be necessary to define &ORIGINAL_SETTINGS with a %GLOBAL statement. Chapter 8 explores %GLOBAL and %LOCAL issues. Also note that PROC OPTSAVE will save all current options settings, enabling PROC OPTLOAD to restore them at a later point.

4.6 Efficiency Considerations

Some function calls generate the same result on every observation:

```
current_date = today();
next_month = intnx("month", today(), +1);
```

Instead of calling the functions on every observation, better technique would call them once:

```
if _n_=1 then do;
   current_date = today();
   next_month = intnx("month", today(), +1);
end;
retain current_date next_month;
```

Still, this approach must check _n_ =1 for each observation. Although the cost is small, %SYSFUNC can eliminate it:

```
retain current_date %sysfunc(today());
retain next_month %sysfunc(intnx(month, %sysfunc(today()), +1));
```

In fact, this approach still calls the TODAY() function twice. Macro language could reduce that to once, with a little more code:

```
%let today = %sysfunc(today());
retain current_date &today;
retain next_month %sysfunc(intnx(month, &today, +1));
```

Is it worth the extra effort? You decide.

4.7 A Final Example: ZIP Codes

In this final %SYSFUNC application, a macro runs PROC FREQ on each of a series of data sets:

```
proc freq data=&dsn;
    tables zipcode;
    title "Zip Codes for &dsn";
run;
```

However, ZIPCODE is character in some data sets and numeric in others. Whenever ZIPCODE is numeric, the macro must detect that fact and add the statement in **bold**:

```
proc freq data=next;
    tables zipcode;
    title "Zip Codes for Next Data Set";
    format zipcode z5.;
run;
```

%SYSFUNC simplifies the task. These statements could appear between the TITLE and RUN statements:

```
%let dataset_id = %sysfunc(open(&dsn));
%let var_id = %sysfunc(varnum(&dataset_id, zipcode));
%let zip_type = %sysfunc(vartype(&dataset_id, &var_id));
%let rc = %sysfunc(close(&dataset_id));
%if &zip_type=N %then %do;
    format zipcode z5.;
%end;
```

In combination, these statements assign &ZIP_TYPE a value of N or C, and they add the FORMAT statement if needed. More specifically, the first statement assigns &DATASET_ID a number that can be used to identify &DSN. The second statement assigns &VAR_ID a number that can be used to identify ZIPCODE within &DSN. The third statement identifies whether ZIPCODE is character or numeric. And the fourth statement closes &DSN.

Alternatives exist. For example, DICTIONARY.COLUMNS contains information about every variable within every SAS data set. But there are advantages to a purely macro-based solution. Section 10.4 will explore those advantages in more detail. Finally, note that more powerful magic can make the macro language disappear entirely from this application. Switch to this FORMAT statement, and all the macro language is unnecessary:

```
format _numeric_ z5.;
```

When ZIPCODE is numeric, the format applies. But when it is character, the FORMAT statement does nothing … no impact but no harm.

4.7.1 Programming Challenge #3

What about more complex situations:

- A TABLES statement lists additional numeric variables that should not use a Z5 format.
- ZIPCODE is still numeric in some data sets and character in others.

How could a FORMAT statement apply to a numeric ZIPCODE but ignore a character ZIPCODE as well as every other numeric variable? Your clue for this problem is that it is possible … a simple FORMAT statement can do the trick.

4.7.2 Solution

Once again, ingenuity makes macro language disappear. Consider these variable lists:

```
dog -- cat            → all variables from DOG through CAT
dog-numeric-cat       → all numeric variables from DOG through CAT
```

The second list works even when DOG and CAT are both character. In fact, all variables in the range might be character so that the list refers to zero variables. This FORMAT statement could apply to no variables in that case:

```
format dog-numeric-cat z5.;
```

That brings us back to the situation where ZIPCODE might be character or numeric:

```
format zipcode-numeric-zipcode z5.;
```

The FORMAT applies to all numeric variables from ZIPCODE through ZIPCODE. If ZIPCODE is character, then the list is empty, and ZIPCODE remains unaffected by the FORMAT statement.

By its nature, %SYSFUNC adds a layer of complexity. Always consider alternatives. Could a DATA step do the job? Is macro language even necessary? Most SAS applications give you a choice.

Chapter 5: CALL SYMPUT

A macro variable that is only two characters long can take on 65,536 different values. When the length of a macro variable reaches 65,534 characters, the number of values reaches a staggering level: 256 ** 65,534. With so many possible values, some of them would certainly cause trouble if they found their way into a program. And CALL SYMPUT is the best tool for causing such trouble. It can assign any conceivable value to a macro variable. Consider this trouble-making combination:

```
data _null_;
    call symput('a', 'NOW; THERE WILL be a #@%&PROBLEM');
run;
%let b = &a;
```

This simple %LET statement resolves into:

```
%let b = NOW; THERE WILL be a #@%&PROBLEM;
```

Although %LET successfully assigns NOW to &B, problems arise:

- The second SAS statement generates an error message because it begins with THERE.
- The macro processor attempts to resolve %&PROBLEM.

It is easy for CALL SYMPUT to assign a troublesome value. Single quotes around the second parameter turn off macro resolution, giving the DATA step great flexibility to assign a multitude of problematic values. Some problems occur naturally, with no attempt to create a troublesome value. That is the focus of the next section.

5.1 Leading and Trailing Blanks

Consider two simple-looking statements:

```
%let a =          250;
%let a = Bob         ;
```

In both cases, the value of &A is three characters long. %LET ignores leading and trailing blanks. Because of that feature this statement is potentially useful:

```
%let a = &a;
```

It would remove any leading or trailing blanks from the value of &A. How do leading or trailing blanks become part of &A to begin with? CALL SYMPUT could easily generate either scenario above:

```
call symput('a', '          250');
call symput('a', 'Bob          ');
```

These statements explicitly include extra blanks within the single quotes. In that sense, they represent an unusual usage of CALL SYMPUT. More commonly, careless usage introduces those extra blanks. The statements below, for example, inadvertently add leading or trailing blanks to &A:

```
call symput('a', n_recipes);
call symput('a', name);
```

The first statement automatically performs a numeric-to-character conversion, transforming N_RECIPES into a twelve-character text string with leading blanks. The second statement transfers the full value of NAME, including any trailing blanks. This issue of extra blanks forms a recurring theme throughout this chapter.

Other tools would have a lot more trouble assigning leading or trailing blanks. Certainly this would be a legal possibility:

```
%let a = %str(          250);
```

However, quoted blanks remain as part of the value of &A. Those quoted blanks would not be removed by coding:

```
%let a = &a;
```

5.2 A Similar Lesson, Using Recursion

Take one more troublesome example. Macro language would normally reject this statement as being "recursive":

```
%let a = %let a = #@%?&;
```

But CALL SYMPUT has no trouble assigning the intended value:

```
call symput ('a', '%let a = #@%?&');
```

Remember, this was our original useful statement:

```
%let a = &a;
```

But that statement now generates the "recursive" result:

```
%let a = %let a = #@%?&;
```

Note that this combination of statements might function differently when embedded in a macro definition. Chapter 2 illustrated a similar case.

The basic lesson, though, is that the single quotes around the second parameter in CALL SYMPUT can assign a percent sign, a single quote, a semicolon, or any other character to a macro variable. Single quotes allow CALL SYMPUT to transfer a virtually limitless set of text values to a macro variable. Some values from that limitless assortment produce troublesome results when the macro variable resolves.

5.3 Test Your Skill

Did the message sink in? Here is a test to find out. In the set of problems below, assume that the statements are used properly within a macro definition.

5.3.1 Programming Challenge #4a

These statements generate Match #2, but they do not generate Match #1. How could this happen?

```
%if "&flower" = "rose" %then %put Match #1;
%let flower = &flower;
%if "&flower" = "rose" %then %put Match #2;
```

5.3.2 Solution

First, consider these DATA step statements:

```
if flower = "rose"    then put 'Match #1';
if flower = "rose   " then put 'Match #2';
```

When either comparison is true, the other must be true as well. When the DATA step compares strings of different lengths, it forces the lengths to match by padding the shorter string with blanks. However, in the macro language, these comparisons are different:

```
%if "&flower" = "rose"    %then %put Match #1;
%if "&flower" = "rose   " %then %put Match #2;
```

When one statement produces a match, the other cannot also match. Macro language looks for an exact match on all characters, including both the quotes and the trailing blanks that are within quotes.

With regard to challenge 4a, suppose CALL SYMPUT creates a variable with trailing blanks:

```
call symput('flower', 'rose   ');
```

In that case, the first statement below resolves into the second statement:

```
%if "&flower" = "rose" %then %put Match #1;
%if "rose   " = "rose" %then %put Match #1;
```

This comparison does not produce a match. However, the next statement changes &FLOWER by removing the trailing blanks:

```
%let flower = &flower;
```

Subsequently, the final statement produces a match:

```
%if "&flower" = "rose" %then %put Match #2;
```

Too easy? Try the second problem.

5.3.3 Programming Challenge #4b

This problem is similar, but the %LET statement in the middle changes. Once again, these statements generate Match #2, but they do not generate Match #1. How could this happen?

```
%if "&flower" = "rose" %then %put Match #1;
%let leaf = &leaf;
%if "&flower" = "rose" %then %put Match #2;
```

5.3.4 Solution

Once you have solved challenge 4a, challenge 4b becomes easier. Somehow, changing the value of &LEAF also changes the value of &FLOWER. The simplest variation sets them equal to one another:

```
data _null_;
   call symput('leaf', 'rose   ');
   call symput('flower', '&leaf');
run;
```

Within the DATA step, single quotes prevent any attempt to resolve &LEAF. But later references to &FLOWER allow the resolution to take place. So the "before" comparison resolves in two steps:

```
%if "&flower" = "rose" %then %put Match #1;
```

Substituting for &FLOWER generates:

```
%if "&leaf" = "rose" %then %put Match #1;
```

Next, substituting for &LEAF generates:

```
%if "rose   " = "rose" %then %put Match #1;
```

As before, the result is a non-match. Then comes the change:

```
%let leaf = &leaf;
```

This statement removes any leading and trailing blanks from &LEAF:

```
%let leaf = rose   ;
```

On the final statement, substituting for &FLOWER generates just four characters:

```
%if "rose" = "rose" %then %put Match #2;
```

One of the keys to solving the problem is recognizing the power of single quotes within CALL SYMPUT. Single quotes prevent any attempts to resolve macro references, allowing live macro triggers to become part of a macro variable.

Still too easy? The theme continues in the next challenge.

5.3.5 Programming Challenge #4c

Now there is no %LET statement between the two comparisons. So how could these statements generate Match #2 but not Match #1?

```
%if "&flower" = "rose" %then %put Match #1;
%if "&flower" = "rose" %then %put Match #2;
```

5.3.6 Solution

In the previous problems, single quotes permitted a live & to become part of a macro variable. In this problem, they permit a live % to become part of a macro variable. Consider this variation:

```
data _null_;
   call symput('flower', '%leaf');
run;
```

Could a macro call generate one result the first time and a different result the second time? When the question takes on that form, the problem becomes feasible. This macro fits the bill:

```
%macro leaf;
   %global ever_done_before;
   %if &ever_done_before=Yes %then rose;
   %else petunia;
   %let ever_done_before=Yes;
%mend leaf;
```

Unless external code somehow alters &EVER_DONE_BEFORE, this macro generates "petunia" the first time it gets called and "rose" every subsequent time. Under these conditions, both of these %IF conditions would be true:

```
%if "&flower" = "rose"    %then %put Flower is petunia.;
%if "&flower" = "petunia" %then %put Flower is rose.;
```

Moreover, it is possible to generate a series of ever-changing values by altering the macro's %LET statement:

```
%let ever_done_before=%eval(&ever_done_before+1);
```

The variations are limited only by your imagination. For example, alter the %LEAF definition along these lines:

```
%if        &ever_done_before=1 %then proc;
%else %if &ever_done_before=2 %then print;
%else %if &ever_done_before=3 %then data;
   . . .
%else %if &ever_done_before=10 %then run;
```

With the complete %IF %THEN logic in place, the macro calls on the left could generate the program on the right:

```
%leaf %leaf %leaf %leaf %leaf;        proc print data=cities;
   %leaf %leaf %leaf %leaf;              var state city pop;
%leaf;                                 run;
```

But coming back to reality for a moment, why would anyone ever do this? Are there any practical applications for a macro that operates differently the first time it gets called? The simplest example might be a single program that:

- Generates a series of reports
- Includes data-generated footnotes
- Numbers the footnotes sequentially
- Uses a single page at the end of all reports to explain the details of the footnotes

Hypothetically, a macro named %FNOTE could generate all the footnotes. Each call to %FNOTE would have to increment a global counter and then add text to the current report to print the counter in a raised position.

5.4 Function Shifts in the Real World

Even simple processes might shift how they function. For example, consider a simple INPUT statement:

```
input amount 8.;
```

As the software searches through eight characters, it must determine whether the characters it finds form a valid numeric. It follows one set of rules until it finds a nonblank. Then it switches gears and follows a different set of rules (because a plus sign, a minus sign, and an embedded blank are now invalid characters). Once a decimal point is found, the rules change again because another decimal point would not be valid. While this description is not all-inclusive (remember that scientific notation is a possibility), it illustrates how a standard process can change each time it encounters another character.

What about macro language? Does it make sense that a macro might change how it operates from one execution to the next?

Recall this situation from Section 4.2. A program generates 100 pages of output. Most of the time, the analyst wants to see only two of those pages to obtain a few key numbers. But occasionally, the other 98 pages are required for further investigation. In that situation, a good programmer would consider creating two output files. Use the .lst file to hold the two key pages, and create a second output file to hold the other 98 pages of backup information. As the program begins creating backup information, add:

```
proc printto print="some_other_file" NEW;
run;
```

Then just before the section creating the two key pages, add:

```
proc printto;
run;
```

Finally, once the key two pages have been created, redirect any remaining output:

```
proc printto print="some_other_file";
run;
```

Leave out the word "NEW" so that additional output gets appended to the existing file.

Before writing the macro, let's embellish the objective. Define a second output file that travels with the program. As we saw in Section 4.2, batch jobs can retrieve the full path to the submitted program:

```
%let path = %sysfunc(getoption(sysin));
```

&PATH is the complete path to the program. Now it's a simple matter to adjust that path:

```
%let path = %substr(&path, 1, %length(&path)-3);
```

By removing the last three characters, &PATH now contains the complete path to the program, minus the letters "sas" at the end. It ends with the dot that used to precede "sas". One final change adds an alternate extension:

```
%let path = &path.backup;
```

Now the program is ready to create a second output file that automatically follows the program path:

```
proc printto print="&path" NEW;
run;
```

Let's wrap that code in a macro and then return to that concept where the macro should operate differently the first time vs. later times it gets called. First, the macro:

```
%macro reroute;
   %global path;
   %if %length(&path)=0 %then %do;
      %let path = %sysfunc(getoption(sysin));
      %let path = %substr(&path, 1, %length(&path)-3);
      %let path = &path.backup;
   %end;
   proc printto print="&path" new;
   run;
%mend reroute;
```

A simple command now reroutes subsequent output to the .backup file:

```
%reroute
```

Once the program reaches the point where it is ready to create the key pages, redirect subsequent output to the .lst file:

```
proc printto print=;
run;
```

The problem becomes more complex if the program shifts several times, alternating between generating important output vs. backup information. Only the first PROC PRINTTO should add the word NEW. But for all subsequent PROC PRINTTO statements, NEW should be eliminated. That enhancement might look like this:

```
%macro reroute;
    %global path;
    %if %length(&path)=0 %then %do;
        %let path = %sysfunc(getoption(sysin));
        %let path = %substr(&path, %length(&path)-3);
        %let path = &path.backup;
        proc printto print="&path" NEW;
    %end;
    %else %do;
        proc printto print="&path";
    %end;
    run;
%mend reroute;
```

NEW is necessary the first time the macro runs. Just in case the same program were to run several times, each run must overwrite the output file from earlier runs. The final version of this macro represents a practical application.

5.5 A Key Issue: Extra Blanks

Many of the CALL SYMPUT issues revolve around the presence of leading or trailing blanks in the second argument. To prevent such issues, programmers often remove the blanks with code along these lines:

```
call symput('leaf', trim(flower));
call symput('tot_amount', trim(left(put(amount, 12.2))));
```

Technically, switching from TRIM to STRIP would remove both leading and trailing blanks, and it would eliminate the need for the LEFT function. In the second statement, the PUT function controls the numeric-to-character conversion, eliminating conversion messages that would otherwise appear on the log. To help with these issues, macro language now contains an expanded version of CALL SYMPUT, named CALL SYMPUTX. Some of its key features center around the second argument:

- If the second argument is character, CALL SYMPUTX automatically removes any leading or trailing blanks.
- If the second argument is numeric, CALL SYMPUTX makes the numeric-to-character conversion automatically but without generating a conversion message in the log. Again, leading or trailing blanks get removed automatically.

The syntax becomes simpler:

```
call symputx('leaf', flower);
call symputx('tot_amount', amount);
```

By allowing CALL SYMPUTX to make the numeric-to-character conversion, the programmer gives up control of the numeric format used to convert to character But it is easy to take back that control:

```
call symputx('tot_amount', put(amount, 12.2));
```

Because the second argument is now character, CALL SYMPUTX still removes leading and trailing blanks. Finally, CALL SYMPUTX contains additional extended features that are unrelated to the second argument. Section 8.4 covers some of those additional features.

CALL SYMPUT plays a role in most macro applications. Always pay attention to leading and trailing blanks, and you'll have much less debugging to perform.

Chapter 6: INTO

If you like CALL SYMPUT, you'll love the INTO : operator in PROC SQL. It also transfers information from a data set to macro variables. But it possesses unique capabilities, such as creating a series of macro variables rather than just one, and extracting data from a collection of observations into a single macro variable. Sections 6.1 through 6.5 illustrate these basic principles, while subsequent material explores more subtle nuances.

6.1 SELECT Executes Immediately

Because SELECT statements execute immediately, this code works:

```
%let tot_sales=;
proc sql noprint;
    %do quarter=1 %to 4;
        select sum(sales) into : q_sales
        from full_year where quarter=&quarter;
```

```
        %let tot_sales = &tot_sales &q_sales;
    %end;
quit;
```

During each iteration of the %DO loop, a SELECT statement populates &Q_SALES. Next, the %LET statement immediately utilizes that value of &Q_SALES. Thus, this section of a macro concatenates the total sales from each quarter into a single macro variable.

6.2 Numeric-to-Character Conversion

Although macro variables hold text strings, INTO : often passes numeric values. This forces SQL to convert numeric values to character. To illustrate, consider this simple example where the incoming data set contains a single observation:

```
data test;
    pi=3.14;
run;

proc sql noprint;
    select pi       into : pi        from test;
    select pi + 2   into : pi_plus_2 from test;
    select ceil(pi) into : ceil_pi   from test;
    select mean(pi) into : mean_pi   from test;
quit;
```

These statements display the results:

```
%put **&pi**;              → **    3.14**
%put **&pi_plus_2**;       → **    5.14**
%put **&ceil_pi**;         → **       4**
%put **&mean_pi**;         → **    3.14**
```

Numeric-to-character conversion takes place even though there is no such message on the log. And PROC SQL makes the conversion using the best8 format, which is different from both CALL SYMPUT and CALL SYMPUTX (best12 format).

6.3 SELECTing Multiple Values

Many INTO : applications select a set of values, rather than a single value. There are two approaches for these cases. Either:

- Create just one macro variable, stringing together information from many incoming observations, or
- Create a set of macro variables

The following example creates a single macro variable. It takes all distinct values for STATE, trims off trailing blanks, puts double quotes around them, and inserts commas between:

```
proc sql noprint;
   select distinct("trim(state)") separated by ', '
   into : state_list
   from popfile;
quit;
```

One possible result:

```
"New Jersey", "New York", "Oregon"
```

This result might be inserted into a later IN operator:

```
where state in (&state_list);
```

The INTO : operator can create a set of macro variables as well:

```
data id_list;
   do idvar=20 to 1 by -1;
      output;
   end;
run;

proc sql noprint;
   select idvar into : v1 - : v20 from id_list;
   %put **&v1**;        →  **20**
   %put **&v2**;        →  **19**
   %put **&v19**;       →  **2**
   %put **&v20**;       →  **1**
quit;
```

INTO : still transforms numeric values into character strings. So where did the leading blanks go? When creating a set of macro variables, the leading blanks are automatically removed. In the unlikely event that the program must preserve these leading blanks, add the NOTRIM option:

```
proc sql noprint;
   select idvar into : v1 - : v20 NOTRIM from id_list;
   %put **&v1**;     →  **    20**
   %put **&v2**;     →  **    19**
   %put **&v19**;    →  **     2**
   %put **&v20**;    →  **     1**
quit;
```

However, be sure to add NOTRIM in the right place. The next variation removes the leading blanks, without generating an error message:

```
proc sql noprint;
    select idvar into : v1 - : v20 from id_list NOTRIM;
    %put **&v1**;        → **20**
    %put **&v2**;        → **19**
    %put **&v19**;       → **2**
    %put **&v20**;       → **1**
quit;
```

6.4 DISTINCT Differences

When SELECT and SELECT DISTINCT create a set of macro variables, the order may be different:

```
proc sql noprint;
    select idvar into : v1 - : v20 from id_list;
    %put **&v1**;        → **20**
    %put **&v2**;        → **19**
    %put **&v19**;       → **2**
    %put **&v20**;       → **1**
    select distinct(idvar) into : v1 - : v20 from id_list;
    %put **&v1**;        → **1**
    %put **&v2**;        → **2**
    %put **&v19**;       → **19**
    %put **&v20**;       → **20**
quit;
```

The first SELECT statement copies the first 20 values of IDVAR into 20 macro variables. But the second SELECT statement has to hold those values aside so it can determine which values are distinct. As a result:

- SELECT DISTINCT assigns values in ascending order
- SELECT assigns values according to their order in the data

6.5 How Many Macro Variables?

What if the number of macro variables does not match the number of data values that PROC SQL selects?

```
proc sql noprint;
   select distinct(trim(state)) into : state1 - : state80
   from popfile;
quit;
```

This program creates as many as 80 macro variables (&STATE1 through &STATE80), depending on the number of STATE values in the incoming data. When the incoming data set contains more than 80 states, only 80 get assigned to macro variables. The rest get ignored. When the incoming data set contains fewer than 80 states, the program creates just the right number of macro variables. (It does not create extra macro variables with null values.) How do you know the number of macro variables that were created? You could try to calculate it. For example, the program could add this statement:

```
select count(distinct(state)) into : n_states from popfile;
```

But this approach has its drawbacks. It must process the data. And the number might be more than 80, even though the number of macro variables is limited to 80. Regardless, this statement is absolutely unnecessary. The software counts for you, using the original SELECT statement. An automatic variable, &SQLOBS, contains the number of macro variables created. So the very next statement inside a macro could be:

```
%do i=1 %to &sqlobs;
```

Or, simply:

```
%let n_states = &sqlobs;
```

6.6 Zero Incoming Observations

A final pitfall: zero incoming observations. This code is trickier than it looks:

```
proc sql noprint;
   select count(*) into : pop_count
        from population;
   select distinct(trim(state))
        into : state_list
        separated by ' '
        from population;
quit;
```

When the incoming data set POPULATION contains zero observations, the two SELECT statements behave differently. The first SELECT statement accurately assigns 0 as the value for &POP_COUNT. But the second SELECT statement does not execute at all. So if &STATE_LIST already has a value (whether null or not), that value remains unchanged. Statistical functions such as COUNT always execute. But data extraction does not execute when the source data set contains zero observations.

6.6.1 Programming Challenge #5

Where does this program go wrong as it attempts to create two macro variables?

```
proc sql noprint;
   select count(distinct(state)) into : n_states
   from popfile;
   select distinct(trim(state)) into : all&n_states
   separated by ' ' from popfile;
quit;
```

Ultimately the intent is to create a single macro variable holding a list of all STATE values in the incoming data. However, the name of the macro variable should reflect the number of STATEs found. For example, if there were 55 STATEs, the macro variable should be named &ALL55.

One feature might appear suspect: creating &N_STATES in one statement and referring to it in the next statement. This is actually not a problem. As shown in Section 6.1, PROC SQL executes its SELECT statements immediately and automatically. The first SELECT statement runs before the second begins. So &N_STATES exists in time. Take a minute to look for the problem, before reading on.

6.6.2 Solution

The problem lies in the value assigned to &N_STATES. A numeric-to-character conversion uses the best8 format to create &N_STATES, assigning it (for example) a value of six blanks followed by 55. So the second SELECT statement sees:

```
     select distinct(trim(state)) into : all       55
     separated by ' ' from popfile;
```

Clearly, this is not a legitimate SELECT statement. Here is one viable fix:

```
proc sql noprint;
   select count(distinct(state)) into : n_states
   from popfile;
   %let n_states = &n_states;
   select distinct(trim(state)) into : all&n_states
   separated by ' ' from popfile;
quit;
```

The %LET statement ignores any leading and trailing blanks and changes &N_STATES to the digits only. Alternatively, ignore &N_STATES and use &SQLOBS instead. The software automatically removes any leading or trailing blanks when assigning a value to &SQLOBS:

```
proc sql noprint;
   select count(distinct(state)) into : n_states
   from popfile;
   select distinct(trim(state)) into : all&sqlobs
   separated by ' ' from popfile;
quit;
```

6.7 An Unusual Application: Separated by Else

Let's revisit a problem from Section 3.3. The data set CUTOFFS holds key information (and is in order by descending SAT_CUTOFF):

Obs	SAT_cutoff	Group_name
1	1200	Honor students
2	900	Regular track
3	300	Challenged

Macro language must use these data values to construct the following program:

```
data student_groups;
   set all_students;
   length group $ 14;
   if score >= 1200 then group='Honor students';
   else if score >= 900 then group='Regular track';
   else if score >= 300 then group='Challenged';
run;
```

Believe it or not, PROC SQL can help! Here, it assembles all the IF / THEN / ELSE statements into a single macro variable:

```
proc sql noprint;
   select 'if score >= ' || put(sat_cutoff, 4.) ||
          " then group='" || trim(group_name) || "';"
          into : logic
          separated by 'else '
          from cutoffs;
run;

data student_groups;
   set all_students;
   length group $ 14;
   &logic
run;
```

The macro variable &LOGIC contains the entire set of IF / THEN / ELSE statements making this a viable solution to the original problem.

6.8 Dictionary Tables

Explaining dictionary tables is beyond the scope of this book. On the other hand, SQL is the only SAS procedure that can access dictionary tables, and a fair number of applications that use INTO : will read from dictionary tables. As a compromise, then, this section illustrates a few dictionary table applications. But it will tread lightly on the syntax, focusing more on the objectives and strategies.

The first example captures the name of every SAS data set in a library. The macro below would need one SELECT statement or the other (not both). The intent is to create a single macro variable holding the names of every SAS data set. The only parameter is the name assigned by an earlier LIBNAME statement:

```
%macro all_datasets (library=);
   %global ds_list;
   proc sql noprint;
      select trim(memname) into : ds_list
         separated by ' '
         from dictionary.tables
         where libname="%upcase(&library)";
      select distinct(trim(memname)) into : ds_list
         separated by ' '
         from dictionary.columns
         where libname="%upcase(&library)";
   quit;
%mend all_datasets;
```

All dictionary tables hold information about the current SAS program or session. DICTIONARY.TABLES contains one observation for each SAS data set, but DICTIONARY.COLUMNS contains one observation for each variable. Therefore, by reading one observation per variable, the second SELECT statement must add DISTINCT (and takes longer to execute as well). If necessary, this macro could examine the variable MEMTYPE to distinguish between data sets, views, and catalogs. That level of complexity extends beyond the focus of this section.

Why do this? What good is a list of all data sets in a library? The list helps when the objective is to process every data set with the same logic. Data cleaning would be a typical application. Here are some steps that might apply to every single data set:

- Find any variables that are always missing.
- Find any variables that have a nonmissing value but never change.
- Get a brief report showing the distribution for each variable.
- Find any character variables that contain leading blanks.

To address the first item on this list (locating variables that are always missing), the following approach would work for a single data set:

```
proc format;
   value there   low-high='There'
                 other='Missing';
   value $there ' '='Missing'
                 other='There';
run;

proc freq data=suspect.dataset;
   tables _all_ / missing;
   format _numeric_ there.
          _character_ $there.;
run;
```

Note that the FORMAT statement requires each data set to contain at least one numeric variable and at least one character variable. Overcoming that limitation is beyond the scope of this section.

Macro enhancements could embellish the results in a number of ways:

- Keep these tables in the .lst file but produce a separate output file listing just those variables that are always missing.

- Expand the process to cover all data sets in the library, adding titles to indicate which data set is the source for each set of tables.

- Add a cutoff parameter. When using a parameter value of 0.98, the macro would report variables that are missing more than 98% of the time.

One final example of using dictionary tables concerns the variable PATIENT_ID. A folder holds many SAS data sets, some of which contain PATIENT_ID. A program must locate which data sets contain PATIENT_ID and then check each one to find any PATIENT_IDs that do not appear on a master list. (A similar, practical objective not addressed here: Verify that PATIENT_ID has the same length, type, label, and format in all data sets.)

The initial objective is to locate all SAS data sets that contain PATIENT_ID and place that list of data set names into a macro variable. DICTIONARY.COLUMNS already identifies every variable in every SAS data set. The trick is to select the proper subset:

- Data sets in just one library
- Variables named PATIENT_ID

A macro might obtain that subset like this:

```
proc sql noprint;
    select trim(memname)
            into : datasets_with_patient_id
            separated by ' '
    from dictionary.columns
            where libname="%upcase(&library)"
            and upcase(name)= 'PATIENT_ID';
quit;
```

Next, process each data set to find patient IDs not on the master list. Because PROC SQL populates &SQLOBS, the macro definition might continue with:

```
%do i=1 %to &sqlobs;
    %let next_dataset = %scan(&datasets_with_patient_id, &i, %str( ));
    proc sort data=&library..&next_dataset (keep=patient_id)
              out=patients NODUPKEY;
        by patient_id;
    run;
    data nomatch;
        merge patients
              master_list (in=in_master);
        by patient_id;
        if in_master=0;
    run;
    proc print data=nomatch;
        var patient_id;
        title "Patient IDs in &next_dataset but NOT in Master_List";
    run;
%end;
```

Each time the loop iterates, the %LET statement selects the name of the next SAS data set that contains PATIENT_ID. From that point, it is straightforward to sort and merge with the master list and to identify the mismatches.

6.9 Extremely Long Lists

Rarely, a list of names becomes so long that it will not fit into a macro variable. Consider this program, for example:

```
proc sql noprint;
    select trim(name)
            into : unformatted_numerics
            separated by ' '
    from dictionary.columns
            where libname="%upcase(&library)"
```

```
            and upcase(memname)="%upcase(&memname)"
            and format=" " and type="num";
    quit;
```

The intent is to extract the names of all unformatted numeric variables from a single SAS data set. Normally, this works smoothly. But data sets exist with tens of thousands of numeric variables. It is possible that the selected string will exceed the longest possible length for a macro variable. What can be done about that?

Let's take a simple case where the objective is to simply subset the variables. The intention would have been to add:

```
    data nums;
        set &library..&memname (keep=&unformatted_numerics);
    run;
```

While the documentation states that the MVARSIZE option can increase the maximum length of a macro variable, the maximum value for MVARSIZE is 64,534 bytes. PROC SQL can still extract the names of all the unformatted numerics, but those names may be too long to fit into a single macro variable. Instead, change the SELECT statement slightly to create an output table:

```
    proc sql noprint;
        create table unformatted_numerics as
        select name
        from dictionary.columns
            where libname="%upcase(&library)"
                and upcase(memname)="%upcase(&memname)"
                and format=" " and type="num";
    quit;
```

Then use CALL EXECUTE to construct the final program:

```
    data _null_;
        call execute("data nums; set &library..&memname (keep=");
        do until (done);
            set unformatted_numerics end=done;
            call execute(name);
        end;
        call execute ("); run;");
        stop;
    run;
```

Notice how the STOP statement is necessary here. By halting the DATA step, it prevents execution of the first CALL EXECUTE an extra time.

You may never encounter a data set with 20,000 variables. But if you do, this workaround can become a vital tool.

6.10 Blanks vs. Nulls

These statements all generate the same results:

```
if state=' ';
if state='      ';
if state='';
```

In most cases, the number of blanks between quotes does not matter. However, the opposite is true for SEPARATED BY. The SELECT clauses below generate different results:

```
proc sql noprint;
    select distinct(trim(state))
           into : one_blank
           separated by ' '
    from popfile;
    select distinct(trim(state))
           into : three_blanks
           separated by '   '
    from popfile;
    select distinct(trim(state))
           into : one_null
           separated by ''
    from popfile;
quit;
```

A series of %PUT statements illustrates the difference:

```
%put **&one_blank**;        →  **Alaska Maine Vermont**
%put **&three_blanks**;     →  **Alaska   Maine   Vermont**
%put **&one_null**;         →  **AlaskaMaineVermont**
```

While it is unusual to need a null separator, it is possible. Section 8.5 contains a realistic example.

INTO : applications cover a tremendously broad spectrum. Whenever the need to extract data overlaps with the need to create macro variables, INTO : comes into play. Expect INTO : to be your ticket OUT OF many programming problems.

Chapter 7: Macro Quoting

Some of life's pleasures are bittersweet. Sometimes you have to pretend to enjoy the meal that your child prepared. Sometimes your appearance in the mirror demands that you visit the gym. And sometimes you have to learn macro language quoting. It's always nice to learn something new, but it's not always pleasant.

7.1 Why Quoting is Necessary

All four statements below run into trouble.

```
%let feature = '&trait';
```

The intent: The macro variable should resolve despite being in single quotes. Actually, single quotes prevent all macro activity, including macro variable resolution.

```
%let heading = title "My Dog"; ;
```

The intent: The first semicolon should be part of the value of &HEADING, and the second should end the %LET statement. Actually, the first semicolon ends the %LET statement.

```
%filmclip (movie=The Good, the Bad and the Ugly)
```

The intent: The comma should be part of the value of &MOVIE. Actually, the comma ends the value assigned to &MOVIE, and the text that follows produces an error condition.

```
%let drink = A&W Root Beer;
```

The intent: The ampersand should be text, part of the value of &DRINK. Actually, SAS will search for a macro variable &W.

In all of these cases, macro language encounters characters that have special meaning, such as the comma, the semicolon, the ampersand, or the single quotes. To succeed, macro language needs to remove the special meaning of those characters, to treat those characters as text rather than as significant symbols.

The DATA step uses quotes for this purpose:

```
name =  Bob ;            →    Bob is symbolic, a variable name
name = 'Bob';            →    Bob is text
reaction = '&;*,-';      →    All five quoted characters are text
```

But macro language does not use quotes for this purpose:

```
%let name =  Bob ;   →   Assigns a three-character value
%let name = 'Bob';   →   Assigns a five-character value
```

Instead, macro language uses functions to treat normally symbolic characters as text:

```
%let feature = %str(%'&trait%');
```

The result: The %STR function (in combination with using %' to refer to single quotes) allows &TRAIT to resolve, while still surrounding it with single quotes.

```
%let heading = %str(title "My Dog";);
```

The result: The %STR function lets macro language treat the first semicolon as text, assigning it as part of the value of &HEADING.

```
%filmclip (movie=%str(The Good, the Bad and the Ugly))
```

The result: The %STR function lets macro language treat the comma as text, making it part of the value of &MOVIE.

```
%let drink = %nrstr(A&W Root Beer);
```

The result: The %NRSTR function lets macro language treat the ampersand as text, allowing &W to become the second and third characters of &DRINK.

The DATA step uses quotes to turn symbolic characters into text. Macro language uses functions instead. As a result, these macro functions are called quoting functions.

7.2 Why Quoting is a Nightmare

Quoting functions were developed over a period of years. Several times, programming situations revealed a need for additional functionality beyond what %STR and %NRSTR provide. Over time, all these features were addressed:

- Quoting words, not just individual characters.
- Execution time quoting vs. compilation time quoting.
- Unquoting.
- Special situations that just couldn't be handled.

Here are a couple of related examples. This first example illustrates the second bullet point, the difference between compilation time quoting and execution time quoting:

```
%macro idaho (state=);
   %if &state=ID %then %do;
      %put State is IDAHO.;
   %end;
%mend idaho;
%idaho (state=NY)
```

The macro works just fine until the day a user wants to process Oregon (state=OR) or Nebraska (state=NE). Either of these statements would generate an error:

```
%if OR=ID %then %do;
%if NE=ID %then %do;
```

Macro language considers both OR and NE (not equal) to be meaningful words, not text. Quoting &STATE can't help because the logic of the macro requires &STATE to resolve. %STR and %NRSTR operate when a macro is compiled, not when it executes. What is needed is the ability to quote later, when a macro executes. So functions such as %BQUOTE and %NRBQUOTE were added to macro language to handle that.

The next situation illustrates the fourth bullet point. Consider this situation where the intent is to generate the equivalent of:

```
title 'My Favorite Candy:  M&Ms';
```

The wrinkle is that the name of the candy is stored in a macro variable:

```
%let ms = Mighty Stupid;
data _null_;
   call symput('candy', 'M&Ms');
run;
title "My Favorite Candy:  &candy";
```

Using double quotes allows &CANDY to resolve. But double quotes cannot suppress the resolution of &MS. So the double-quoted title becomes:

```
title "My Favorite Candy:  MMighty Stupid";
```

Yet another quoting function handles the situation. When a macro executes, %SUPERQ masks every special character (as well as mnemonic operators such as OR and NE):

```
title "My Favorite Candy:  %superq(candy)";
```

More situations to handle = more quoting functions = more complications. The programming analogy might be:

- Write a complex program.
- Modify the program to handle unforeseen problems.
- Repeat the second step multiple times.

With each iteration, the program gets messier and messier. By the time you are done, your program works. But you might be saying to yourself, "If I had known about all these issues when I started, I might have written this differently." That is the evolution of quoting, over time.

7.3 What Quoting Really Does

Technically, quoting functions change the symbolic characters, storing them using a different bit pattern. When it is time to turn generated text into SAS language statements, macro language magically figures out that it is time to change the characters back to their original bit pattern. As an example, consider this program:

```
data _null_;
   three_semicolons = ';;;';
   quoted_version = ";%str(;);";
   put three_semicolons $hex6.    →  3B3B3B
       quoted_version   $hex6.;   →  3B3B3B
run;
```

Even though one variable contains a quoted semicolon, the software unquotes it before the PUT statement writes it. By the time the DATA step executes, both variables contain the same characters. So how do we know that the quoting function does anything at all? Writing out a quoted character with a %PUT statement sheds some light:

```
%let quoted_semi = %str(;);

%put &quoted_semi;

%put _user_;
```

The first %PUT statement simply writes a semicolon, as if no quoting had occurred. But the second shows the impact of quoting. When writing user-created macro variables with automatic variables, such as _USER_, quoting remains in place. Instead of writing out a semicolon, the second %PUT statement writes out three unprintable characters. (Unprintable characters typically display as an empty box.) While all three are unprintable, internally they are actually different. Why three characters instead of one? %STR uses one unprintable character to show when quoting begins, a second one to hold the quoted semicolon, and a third to show when quoting ends.

There is other evidence that quoting really changes characters internally. For example, the software doesn't always figure out when it should unquote a character. Be alert for this combination of conditions:

- It looks like nothing is wrong with the program, but
- There is an error message, and
- The program contains characters quoted by macro language.

This combination indicates that the software failed to unquote a quoted character. Sending a password to SQL is one case that typically encounters this issue. Here is the section of a SAS statement that specifies the password:

```
' " my_secret_password " '
```

When a macro variable holds the password, this combination would not work:

```
%let password=my_secret_password;
' " &password " '
```

The single quotes suppress macro activity, preventing the resolution of &PASSWORD. The %STR function helps by quoting the single quotes but not the ampersand. It allows &PASSWORD to resolve:

```
%str(%' " &password " %')
```

Yet the software generates an error message because it cannot convert the quoted characters back to their original form in time for SQL to properly parse the expression. Luckily, unquoting the entire expression converts the characters back to their proper form in time:

```
%unquote(%str(%' " &password " %'))
```

7.4 Peeking Inside the Black Box of Quoting

It's time for a little magic. Suppose we wanted to break the secret code of macro language quoting, and figure out which bit patterns SAS uses to store quoted characters. Could we do that? Could we even approach the problem? The rest of this section will trick the software into revealing its secrets.

Will this be interesting? It depends on your point of view. It's decidedly boring to determine which bit patterns quoting uses. But it's much more interesting if you think of it this way. Let's open up the black box of macro language quoting to explore parts of the process that we were never meant to see.

Here is one plan to pry open the quoting process:

- Transfer each character to a macro variable.
- Quote the macro variable.
- Print the quoted version.

As the example with three semicolons demonstrates, this plan faces serious obstacles. The software is built to unquote characters before we can examine them. Here is one more attempt that still fails:

```
data _null_;
   semicolon = ';';
   put semicolon $hex2.;          → 3B
   call symput ('macrovar', semicolon);
   call execute('%let macrovar = %superq(macrovar);');
   quoted_semicolon=symget('macrovar');
   put quoted_semicolon $hex2.;   → 3B
run;
```

As noted in Section 3.4, when CALL EXECUTE generates macro language statements, those statements execute immediately. So in executing the DATA step, the software runs CALL SYMPUT, then executes the %LET statement, and then continues the DATA step, using SYMGET to assign a value to QUOTED_SEMICOLON. %SUPERQ quotes any and all special characters, including a semicolon. But as SYMGET retrieves &MACROVAR, it unquotes the semicolon before we can examine it. Can we conjure up some more powerful magic to overcome this feature of SYMGET?

The strength of the software also proves to be its undoing, forcing it to reveal its quoting secrets. We will approach the problem from the opposite direction. For each character:

- Display it in hex format.
- Transfer it to a macro variable.
- Unquote the macro variable.
- Display the unquoted value, both as a character and in hex format.

In a nutshell, the software does an excellent job of unquoting characters. So let it unquote every character, and we can examine which ones change. Using hindsight, here are the results for one selected character:

```
data _null_;
   character_in = '0E'x;
   call symput ('macrovar', character_in));
   length character_out $ 1;
   character_out = symget('macrovar');
   hexcode_out = put(character_out, $hex2.);
   put hexcode_out              → 3B
       character_out;           → ;
run;
```

This program starts with hex code 0E, and it demonstrates that this is the bit pattern that macro language uses to hold a quoted semicolon. The key steps include:

- CALL SYMPUT copies into a macro variable the character represented by hex code 0E.
- SYMGET retrieves that macro variable, automatically unquotes it, and stores the result as the DATA step variable CHARACTER_OUT.
- The PUT statement reveals that the unquoted character is a semicolon, with hex code 3B instead of 0E.

In short, this program demonstrates that unquoting hex code 0E turns it into a semicolon. But why start with 0E? How did we know it would turn into a semicolon? The answer is to write a program to find all characters affected by unquoting. For example:

```
data _null_;
   file print notitles;
   put '**************************************************';
   do _i_=0 to 255;
      hexcode_in = put(_i_, hex2.);
      call symput('macrovar', input(hexcode_in, $hex2.));
      length hexcode_out $ 2;
      hexcode_out = put(symget('macrovar'), $hex2.);
```

```
      if hexcode_in ne hexcode_out then do;
         print_char = input(hexcode_out, $hex2.);
         put hexcode_in= hexcode_out= print_char=;
      end;
   end;
   put '**************************************************';
run;
```

This program transfers every possible character to a macro variable, unquotes it, and checks whether unquoting changes the value. Here is the list of those that change, for one operating system:

```
**************************************************
hexcode_in=01 hexcode_out=20 print_char=
hexcode_in=02 hexcode_out=20 print_char=
hexcode_in=03 hexcode_out=20 print_char=
hexcode_in=04 hexcode_out=20 print_char=
hexcode_in=05 hexcode_out=20 print_char=
hexcode_in=06 hexcode_out=20 print_char=
hexcode_in=07 hexcode_out=20 print_char=
hexcode_in=08 hexcode_out=20 print_char=
hexcode_in=0B hexcode_out=5E print_char=^
hexcode_in=0E hexcode_out=3B print_char=;
hexcode_in=0F hexcode_out=26 print_char=&
hexcode_in=10 hexcode_out=25 print_char=%
hexcode_in=11 hexcode_out=27 print_char='
hexcode_in=12 hexcode_out=22 print_char="
hexcode_in=13 hexcode_out=28 print_char=(
hexcode_in=14 hexcode_out=29 print_char=)
hexcode_in=15 hexcode_out=2B print_char=+
hexcode_in=16 hexcode_out=2D print_char=-
hexcode_in=17 hexcode_out=2A print_char=*
hexcode_in=18 hexcode_out=2F print_char=/
hexcode_in=19 hexcode_out=3C print_char=<
hexcode_in=1A hexcode_out=3E print_char=>
hexcode_in=1C hexcode_out=3D print_char==
hexcode_in=1D hexcode_out=7C print_char=|
hexcode_in=1E hexcode_out=2C print_char=,
hexcode_in=1F hexcode_out=7E print_char=~
hexcode_in=7F hexcode_out=23 print_char=#
**************************************************
```

The values of PRINT_CHAR might look vaguely familiar. They form the list of all characters affected by quoting. Also note how most of the hex codes are sequential. But the last line skips from hex code 1F to hex code 7F. That is no accident. Macro language added the pound sign as a special character many years after the others on the list, when SAS 9.3 introduced it as the equivalent of a macro language IN operator.

There is no guarantee that these mappings apply across operating systems or even across releases of the software for the same operating system. But a guarantee is unnecessary … just rerun the program.

7.5 The Final Word on Quoting

Quoting is as much mystical as it is intuitive. You may (or may not) be able to predict the results of these tests:

```
%let food=fruit;
%let fruit=apple;

%let t1 = %nrbquote(&&&food);        → apple
%let t2 = %str(&&)&food;             → &fruit
%let t3 = &t2;                       → &fruit
%let t4 = %unquote(&t2);             → apple

%let ampersand = &&;                 → &
%let t5 = &ampersand.fruit;          → apple
%let t6 = &&%nrbquote(&food);        → &fruit
%let t7 = &t6;                       → &fruit
%let t8 = &&%str(fruit);             → &fruit
%let t9 = &&fruit;                   → apple
```

It is always important to test your code. Test it more when it involves macro quoting. In addition to the %PUT _USER_ statement mentioned earlier, the SYMBOLGEN option can also help. It displays unquoted values, but it also mentions on the log when macro variables have been unquoted for printing purposes.

Chapter 8: %LOCAL vs. %GLOBAL

Global variables. Local variables that automatically vanish. A compendium of rules that depend on which tool creates a macro variable. Why do we need these complications?

8.1 Why Think %Locally?

Why should this be an issue? Why not just make all macro variables global, and eliminate the related complications? After all, in a %GLOBAL world, %LET would have the same effect whether it appears inside or outside of a macro. In this example, %UPPER affects the one (and only) %GLOBAL version of &SIZES2:

```
%let sizes1 = Small Medium Large;
%let sizes2 = Small Medium Large;
%let sizes1 = %upcase(&sizes1);
%macro upper;
    %let sizes2 = %upcase(&sizes2);
%mend upper;
%upper
%put &sizes1;     → SMALL MEDIUM LARGE
%put &sizes2;     → SMALL MEDIUM LARGE
```

But when local variables exist, the result changes:

```
%let sizes1 = Small Medium Large;
%let sizes2 = Small Medium Large;
%let sizes1 = %upcase(&sizes1);
%macro upper;
   %local sizes2;
   %let sizes2 = %upcase(&sizes2);
%mend upper;
%upper
%put &sizes1;      → SMALL MEDIUM LARGE
%put &sizes2;      → Small Medium Large
```

Within %UPPER, the %UPCASE function works on the local version of &SIZES2. But the %PUT statement works on the global version. The local version disappears as soon as %UPPER finishes executing.

So what are the benefits of this added complexity? The first benefit has already been mentioned in passing. When a macro finishes executing, cleanup occurs automatically. Its symbol table vanishes. Removing a %GLOBAL macro variable actually takes more work:

```
%symdel sizes1;
```

But the primary advantage of creating %LOCAL symbol tables is that many programmers can write many macros independently of one another. Programmers need not worry about which macro variable names are already in use by other macros because changes to variables in one local symbol table do not affect any other symbol tables.

8.2 Creating Symbol Tables and Macro Variables

When does the software create a local symbol table? Not until it is absolutely necessary. None of these conditions are sufficient:

- Defining a macro
- Executing a macro that works with only global variables
- Executing CALL SYMPUT.

This test sheds further light on the subject:

```
%macro test;
   %put _local_;
   %local abc;
   %put _local_;
%mend test;
%test
```

Only the second %PUT statement writes any messages. The local table does not exist until the %LOCAL statement executes.

When macros call macros, multiple symbol tables exist, and complications arise. How can you create a macro variable in the proper table? When retrieving a macro variable, how do you retrieve the proper variable when two symbol tables both contain a macro variable having the same name?

To navigate the complications, master a few basic principles:

- The effects of a %GLOBAL statement
- The effects of a %LOCAL statement
- The search process that the software employs to locate an existing macro variable.

```
%global abc;
```

This statement means, "If the global symbol table contains a macro variable &ABC, do nothing. But if not, create &ABC in the global symbol table, assigning it a null value." Suppose these two statements were to appear within a macro definition:

```
%global abc;
%let abc=;
```

Is the second statement really needed? Won't the %GLOBAL statement create &ABC with a null value? Actually, the second statement might be vital. If the %GLOBAL statement creates &ABC, the %LET statement is not needed. However, the %GLOBAL statement does nothing if &ABC already exists in the global symbol table. In fact, &ABC might already exist if a program calls the same macro twice. For the second execution, the %LET statement might be necessary to reset &ABC to a null value.

```
%local abc;
```

This statement means, "If the local symbol table (for the macro that contains this statement) contains &ABC, do nothing. But if not, create &ABC in that local symbol table, assigning it a null value." %LOCAL statements can appear only within a macro definition.

The only function of the %LOCAL and %GLOBAL statements is to create a macro variable if it does not already exist. In that light, this program is perfectly valid:

```
%macro my_way;
    %global abc;
    %local abc;
%mend my_way;
```

The macro creates &ABC in the global symbol table, and it then creates another macro variable (also named &ABC) in the local symbol table. But what if we were to reverse the order?

```
%macro your_ways;
    %local abc;
    %global abc;
%mend your_ways;
```

Can you see the error in %YOUR_WAYS? Perhaps this code should run error-free, but it doesn't. Evidently, this combination fears that you are misunderstanding how the %GLOBAL statement works, and it thinks you are attempting to move a local variable to the global table. So to prevent this misunderstanding from generating an incorrect result, this code generates an error instead. Don't attempt to create a global variable when the local symbol table already contains a macro variable with the same name. Subterfuge will fail. This program generates the same error:

```
%macro a;
    %local abc;
    %b
%mend a;
%macro b;
    %global abc;
%mend b;
%a
```

The final basic principle is the search process. What happens if a macro refers to &ABC, and both the local and global symbol tables contain &ABC? The program retrieves the local version. The software searches for &ABC in the local table first and then in the global table. It uses the first &ABC it finds. (In the case of macros calling macros, the search order begins with the innermost local table and ends with the global table.)

8.2.1 Programming Challenge #6

With these principles in mind, find the fundamental flaw in this macro:

```
%macro sequels (movie);
    %do m=1 %to 5;
        proc print data=all.movies;
            where movie = "&movie &m";
            title "Movie:   &movie &m";
        run;
    %end;
%mend sequels;
```

Clearly, some values of &MOVIE will have fewer than four sequels. But no harm is done by a WHERE statement that retrieves zero observations. So where is the flaw?

8.2.2 Solution

Even though the code runs error-free, it still embodies a fundamental flaw. The macro is missing a %LOCAL statement, creating &M in its local symbol table. Consider the consequences if another macro were to call this macro. If the calling macro contains a macro variable &M, even if it were defined with a %LOCAL statement within the calling macro, %SEQUELS would change &M in the calling macro's symbol table. Omitting the %LOCAL statement within %SEQUELS makes it unsafe for another macro to call the %SEQUELS macro. For example, consider this relatively simple macro that harbors the same flaw:

```
%macro varlist;
    %do m=1 %to 3;
        var&m
    %end;
%mend varlist;
```

Try pairing such a simple macro with a variation of %SEQUELS:

```
%macro sequels (movie);
    %do m=1 %to 5;
        proc print data=all.movies;
            where movie = "&movie &m";
            title "Movie:   &movie &m";
            var %varlist;
        run;
    %end;
%mend sequels;
```

Now executing %SEQUELS generates an infinite loop. %VARLIST utilizes &M from the local symbol table of %SEQUELS. Thus this loop never finishes:

```
%do m=1 %to 5;
```

Don't write dangerous macros. Define your %LOCAL variables!

8.3 Symbol Tables with CALL SYMPUT

CALL SYMPUT complicates matters when it creates a macro variable. It follows two rules to determine whether a macro variable needs to be created and which symbol table to use:

- Search for an existing macro variable that has the proper name. If it exists, use the existing variable.

- If the target macro variable does not exist, create it but do not create a symbol table. Instead, place it in the closest existing symbol table.

This program illustrates those rules:

```
%macro where_did_it_go;
   data _null_;
      call symput("before", "??");
   run;
   %local abc;
   data _null_;
      call symput("after", "????");
   run;
   %put _user_;
%mend where_did_it_go;
%where_did_it_go
```

The first CALL SYMPUT writes &BEFORE to the global table because the local table does not exist yet. Next, executing the %LOCAL statement forces creation of the local symbol table. The second CALL SYMPUT writes &AFTER to the suddenly available local symbol table.

Many macros avoid this complication automatically:

```
%macro typical (dsn=, n=);
```

Once a macro begins to execute, parameters on the %MACRO statement force creation of a local symbol table. If an embedded CALL SYMPUT must create a macro variable, a local symbol table is available.

Next, examine a deceptively simple macro. Which symbol table will CALL SYMPUT use when creating &VAR1 through &VAR5?

```
%macro it_depends;
   %do w=1 %to 5;
      data _null_;
         call symput("var&w", "&w");
      run;
   %end;
%mend it_depends;
%it_depends
```

The answer is, "It depends." Sometimes CALL SYMPUT uses the global table, and sometimes it uses the local table. How can that be?

As the macro begins to execute, there is no local symbol table. The key question becomes: Does the global symbol table already contain &W? If it does:

- The %DO loop iterates the global variable.
- There is no local symbol table.
- CALL SYMPUT must use the global symbol table.

But if the global symbol table does not already contain &W:

- The %DO loop is forced to create &W, creating a local symbol table to hold it.
- CALL SYMPUT uses the local symbol table.

Even though the complete macro definition is in plain sight, there is no way to know ahead of time which symbol table CALL SYMPUT will use.

One last programming feature affects the creation of a local symbol table. Section 6.5 noted how PROC SQL automatically creates macro variables. As part of that process, PROC SQL always uses the local symbol table; if that table does not yet exist, the presence of PROC SQL forces the software to create it. And as this program illustrates, creation of that local table affects CALL SYMPUT's macro variables:

```
%macro which_table;
   data _null_;
      call symput('before', 'before SQL');   → to global table
   run;
   proc sql noprint;
      create table new as select * from old;
   quit;
   data _null_;
      call symput ('after', 'after SQL');   → to local table
   run;
   %put _user_;
%mend which_table;
%which_table
```

The first CALL SYMPUT writes to the global table because there is no local table. When PROC SQL runs, the software creates a local symbol table. Therefore, the second CALL SYMPUT writes to the suddenly available local table.

8.4 Symbol Tables with CALL SYMPUTX

Section 5.5 introduced CALL SYMPUTX, the expanded version of CALL SYMPUT. This section revisits CALL SYMPUTX, focusing on its ability to control the symbol table that holds its output.

CALL SYMPUTX supports a third parameter:

```
call symputx("varname", "value", F/G/L);
```

When the third parameter is F, the software tries to Find an existing macro variable with the proper name. This is the default action, the same behavior that CALL SYMPUT uses. When the third parameter is G, there is no search for an existing macro variable. The software automatically stores &VARNAME in the Global symbol table. When the third parameter is L, the software uses the closest available Local symbol table. Again, the software skips any attempt to locate &VARNAME in an existing symbol table.

8.5 Choosing the Source Table

With a system of macros calling macros calling macros, suppose you would like to retrieve &P from the global symbol table. There may or may not be other &P values in various local symbol tables. How do you retrieve &P from the global symbol table, regardless of the contents of any local symbol tables?

The first step is to check to see whether &P exists. If so, where does it exist? Any of these statements can help:

```
%if %symglobl(P) %then %do;
%if %symlocal(P) %then %do;
%if %symexist(P) %then %do;
```

These statements check respectively whether &P exists in the global symbol table, whether it exists in a local symbol table, and whether it exists at all. All three functions return a 1 when the variable exists and a 0 when it doesn't.

If &P exists in the global symbol table, its value is available ... even if another &P exists in a local symbol table. But retrieving it takes more work.

The SASHELP.VMACRO data set tracks all existing macro variables in all symbol tables, and that mapping is available to both the DATA step and PROC SQL. NAME, SCOPE, and VALUE are all stored for each macro variable. Here is some code that could appear within a macro:

```
%local global_version_of_p;
data _null_;
    set sashelp.vmacro;
    where name='P' and scope='GLOBAL';
    call symputx('global_version_of_p', value);
run;
```

Notice a few details. First, VALUE has a length of 200. For shorter macro variables that contain trailing blanks, SASHELP.VMACRO does not track how many trailing blanks were in the original value. Also note that CALL SYMPUTX removes all leading and trailing blanks. Finally, what if the original macro variable were longer than 200 characters? In that case, its value gets split into 200-character chunks, and it occupies multiple observations in SASHELP.VMACRO. The variable OFFSET tracks how to reassemble the pieces:

Scope	Name	Offset	Value
GLOBAL	P	0	First 200 chars of P in Global Symbol Table
GLOBAL	P	200	Chars 201-400 of P in Global Symbol Table
GLOBAL	P	400	Chars 401-600 of P in Global Symbol Table
GLOBAL	P	600	Chars 601-800 of P in Global Symbol Table

When OFFSET is 0, VALUE contains the first 200 characters of a macro variable. When OFFSET is 200, VALUE contains the next 200 characters. Think of OFFSET as the number of characters to move to the right, before placing VALUE into a portion of a macro variable. While a DATA step could reassemble the pieces, PROC SQL makes it look (relatively) easy:

```
proc sql noprint;
    select value into : global_version_of_p separated by ''
    from sashelp.vmacro
    where name='P' and scope='GLOBAL';
quit;
```

Notice how SEPARATED BY uses a null character, not a blank. As shown in Section 6.10, a null separator strings all the VALUEs together without inserting any blanks between them.

8.6 A Persisting Impact

When a macro finishes executing, its symbol table vanishes. What if the program needs some of that information? What tools or techniques allow a macro to contribute to a program, even after the macro completes?

The simplest technique is to create global macro variables. Both a %GLOBAL statement and CALL SYMPUTX play a role here. A second approach is to generate text instead of saving macro variables. If a macro has generated some text, those words remain part of the program after the macro ends. Chapter 10 will explore this approach in greater detail. For now, we will examine a different technique: passing the name (rather than the value) of a global macro variable as a macro parameter.

Here is the background for this example. A macro adds "Jack" at the beginning of several macro variables. Before the macro begins, these global variables exist:

```
%let var1 = be nimble;
%let var5 = be quick;
%let var8 = jump over the candlestick;
```

The straightforward approach skips defining a macro:

```
%let var1 = Jack &var1;    →  Jack be nimble
%let var5 = Jack &var2;    →  Jack be quick
%let var8 = Jack &var3;    →  Jack jump over the candlestick
```

Clearly, this is the right approach for such a simple objective. But this is just a simplified example, in order to illustrate a point. If a macro were to approach the same problem, it might encounter difficulties:

```
%macro add_jack (firstvar=, secondvar=, thirdvar=);
   %let firstvar  = Jack &firstvar;
   %let secondvar = Jack &secondvar;
   %let thirdvar  = Jack &thirdvar;
%mend add_jack;
%add_jack (firstvar=&var1, secondvar=&var5, thirdvar=&var8)
```

While the macro can add "Jack" in the right places, it has difficulty replacing &VAR1, &VAR5, and &VAR8 in the global symbol table. Instead, it replaces &FIRSTVAR, &SECONDVAR, and &THIRDVAR in the local symbol table. A better approach would pass the names of the global macro variables rather than their values. Here is one possibility:

```
%macro add_jack (firstvar=, secondvar=, thirdvar=);
   %let &firstvar  = Jack &&&firstvar;
   %let &secondvar = Jack &&&secondvar;
   %let &thirdvar  = Jack &&&thirdvar;
%mend add_jack;
%add_jack (firstvar=var1, secondvar=var5, thirdvar=var8)
```

Of course, this approach adds complexities such as using three ampersands. But it successfully generates %LET statements that change existing global macro variables. And this key technique makes it work: passing the name of a global macro variable.

Chapter 9: Arithmetic

The basics may bore you, but the details will delight you.

9.1 Basic Rules

The %LET statement automatically ignores arithmetic:

```
%let total =  3 * 5   ;
```

Here, &TOTAL is five characters long, and the third character is an asterisk. As usual, leading and trailing blanks are ignored. For the %LET statement to perform arithmetic, it must apply a function:

```
%let total = %eval(3 * 5);          → 15
%let total = %sysevalf(3 * 5);      → 15
```

The %EVAL function performs integer arithmetic, dropping any remainders:

```
%let total = %eval(10 / 4);    → 2
%let total = %eval(2.5 * 4);   → error, decimal points not allowed
%let total = %eval(10./4.);    → error, decimal points not allowed
```

Permissible variations include negative integers and parentheses to influence the order of operations:

```
%let total = %eval(-10 / (4 + 3));    → -1
```

The %SYSEVALF function was invented later, to compute using decimal fractions:

```
%let total = %sysevalf(10 / 4);    → 2.5
%let total = %sysevalf(2.5 * 4);   → 10
```

Finally, %SYSEVALF supports a second parameter, indicating an operation to perform on the calculated result. Some examples:

```
%let total = %sysevalf(-10/3, floor);    → -4
%let total = %sysevalf(-10/3, ceil);     → -3
%let total = %sysevalf(-10/3, int);      → -3
%let total = %sysevalf(-10/3, Boolean);  →  1
```

Boolean transformations return 0 or 1, depending on the result calculated by %SYSEVALF:

0: the result was 0 or missing

1: the result was any other value

Boolean transformation can prevent division by zero. For example:

```
%if %sysevalf(&denominator, Boolean) %then
%let ratio = %sysevalf((&numerator) / (&denominator));
```

The first %SYSEVALF returns either a 1 (which %IF interprets as "true") or a 0 (which %IF interprets as "false"). And 1 corresponds exactly to the cases where division is possible: a nonmissing, nonzero denominator.

Take a quick challenge before moving on. Why use extra parentheses around &NUMERATOR and &DENOMINATOR? How is it possible that removing the parentheses would generate a different result?

The simplest answer is that one or both macro variables might contain an expression rather than a hard-coded value. Consider this combination:

```
%let numerator = 5 + 10;
%let denominator = 10 + 5;
```

Now removing parentheses changes the result:

```
(&numerator) / (&denominator)  →  (5 + 10) / (10 + 5)  →   1
&numerator  /  &denominator    →   5 + 10  /  10 + 5   →  11
```

9.2 Truth in Numbers, Expressions, and Comparisons

Both %EVAL and %SYSEVALF can evaluate expressions as being true or false, replacing a true expression with 1 and a false expression with 0:

```
%let value   = %eval(FAME > LOVE);        → 0
%let store   = %sysevalf(5&10);           → 1
%let message = %sysevalf(.S|.O|.S);       → 0
```

Because "F" is less than "L", the first comparison is false and %EVAL returns 0. Because 5 is true and 10 is also true (0 and missing are the only false numerics), the second statement returns 1. Because all special missing values are false, the third statement returns 0. (Note that | is another way of expressing the word OR.)

Previous examples noted how %IF interprets 1 as true and 0 as false. As with the SAS language, macro language interprets a broad range of numeric values as true or false. %IF interprets integer values only, and 0 is the only false value. Here is a brief macro to demonstrate:

```
%macro true_false (value);
    %if &value %then %put &value is True.;
    %else %put &value is False.;
%mend true_false;
```

```
%true_false (0)      → 0 is False.
%true_false (3)      → 3 is True.
%true_false (-5)     → -5 is True.
%true_false (1.)     → Error, decimal points are not permitted
%true_false ()       → Error, no %if condition specified
%true_false (.)      → Error, . is not a missing value in macro language
```

These results have practical implications for common programming statements. Both of these statements can be simplified:

```
%if %index(&string1, &string2) > 0 %then %do;
%if %length(&list) > 0 %then %do;
```

Both %INDEX and %LENGTH return nonnegative integers. %IF interprets 0 as false and other integers as true. Thus these replacements are possible:

```
%if %index(&string1, &string2) %then %do;
%if %length(&list) %then %do;
```

If the software determines that math should be performed, it will do so even if no functions are present. In these situations, the %EVAL function gets applied automatically to every mathematical expression:

```
%do i = &a / 2 %to 3 + &b;
%let word5 = %scan(&var_list, 1+4);
```

The automatic %EVAL saves the clumsiness of having to code:

```
%do i = %eval(&a / 2) %to %eval(3 + &b);
%let word5 = %scan(&var_list, %eval(1+4));
```

Note that %EVAL (not %SYSEVALF) is being applied. Therefore, the software performs integer arithmetic.

How does the software "know" when to perform math, even without an explicit %EVAL function? Both the %DO loop and the %SCAN function require numeric values. So the software helps out by performing the math automatically.

Technically, %IF %THEN statements invoke %EVAL every time. So adding %EVAL here is unnecessary:

```
%if %eval(3 + 2) > 10 %then %do;
```

But what does that mean in practice? What steps does %EVAL take to evaluate a %IF condition? Begin with a few simpler comparisons:

```
%if 5 > 10 %then %do;

%if 3 + 2 > 10 %then %do;

%if 4 miles < 20 miles %then %do;
```

These statements are straightforward:

- The first statement makes a numeric comparison. Because 5 is less than 10, the %IF condition is false.
- The second statement performs the math and then makes the same numeric comparison.
- The third statement contains no math. However, there are characters within the comparison. Therefore, the software makes a character comparison. Because "4" is greater than "2", the comparison is false.

As the expressions become more complex, they reveal details about how the software applies %EVAL to the entire %IF comparison. Consider a few more complex statements:

```
%if 1 + 3 < 3bc %then %do;

%if 1 + 3 < 5bc %then %do;

%if 1 + 3 miles < 5 miles %then %do;
```

Hard-coding %EVAL isn't needed because the software is invoking it anyway. So what do these statements mean?

- For the first statement, %EVAL notices that there is math to perform. It performs the math, and then it notices there are characters within the comparison. So it performs a character comparison, finds that "4" is greater than "3" and identifies the overall comparison as false.
- For the second statement, %EVAL again performs the math. The result still contains characters, so a character comparison is made. Because "4" is less than "5", the comparison is true.
- In the final statement, %EVAL notices that there is math to perform. However, it attempts to perform math on the entire string "1 + 3 miles". Because there is no way to perform math on "miles", this statement generates an error message.

In summary, %EVAL is taking these steps to process a %IF comparison:

- Inspect each side of the comparison separately. If any mathematical operators appear, apply %EVAL to that entire side.
- Examine the result. If only integers remain, perform a numeric comparison. But if any non-integers remain, perform a character comparison.

When conducting that initial inspection, mathematical operators (not integers) trigger the software to invoke %EVAL for that side of the comparison. So this is a perfectly valid assignment statement:

```
%let rank = A-1;
```

However, this statement always generates an error message:

```
%if &rank = A-1 %then %do;
```

The minus sign triggers %EVAL to attempt arithmetic on A-1, generating the error. One way to suppress that attempt is to add double quotes to the comparison. This statement eliminates the error and performs a character comparison:

```
%if "&rank" = "A-1" %then %do;
```

But remove the quotes when math should be performed. This group of statements generates Match #1 but not Match #2:

```
%let a = 3 + 4;
%let b = 4 + 3;
%if &a = &b %then %put Match #1;
%if "&a" = "&b" %then %put Match #2;
```

The quotes prevent the math from being performed, resulting in an inequality. But removing the quotes allows %IF conditions to perform math, resulting in equality. Similarly, these statements also produce Match #1 but not Match #2:

```
%let vision = 20-20;
%let split = 50-50;
%if &vision = &split %then %put Match #1;
%if "&vision" = "&split" %then %put Match #2;
```

Finally, this statement performs the math, which is likely not the right action:

```
%if &lottery_numbers = 1 - 6 - 28 - 39 - 43 - 44 %then %do;
```

Other pitfalls exist. In particular, beware of decimal points. Decimal points are so lethal to %EVAL that even this statement would generate an error message:

```
%do i=1. %to 5.;
```

With no decimal points, this statement performs a numeric comparison and writes First:

```
%if 22 + 5 > 4 %then %put First;
```

However, because of the decimal point, this statement performs a character comparison and writes nothing:

```
%if 22 + 5 > 4. %then %put Second;
```

9.2.1 Programming Challenge #7

At last it is time to dig into a macro that is a whopping 20 lines long. This macro (%BUBBLY) reorders a list of four words alphabetically. For example:

```
%let list = some list of words;
%bubbly (list)
%put &list;   → list of some words

%let yoda_speak = this is too clever;
%bubbly (yoda_speak)
%put &yoda_speak;   → clever is this too
```

The macro appears below:

```
%macro bubbly (macvar);
    %local i j changes dummy
           word1 word2 word3 word4;
    %do i=1 %to 4;
        %let word&i = %scan(&&&macvar,&i,%str( ));
    %end;
    %do %until (&changes=No);
        %let changes=No;
        %do i=1 %to 3;
            %let j=%eval(&i+1);
            %if &&word&j < &&word&i %then %do;
                %let changes=Yes;
                %let dummy = &&word&i;
                %let word&i = &&word&j;
                %let word&j = &dummy;
            %end;
        %end;
    %end;
    %let &macvar=&word1 &word2 &word3 &word4;
%mend bubbly;
```

The macro compares the first word to the second, the second word to the third, and the third word to the fourth. Any time the words are not in order, the macro switches them. Finally, if any switches were made, the macro repeats the entire process.

Your mission is to break it using logic, not syntax. Generate an incorrect result, without generating an error message. More specifically, invent a set of four different text strings. But the order of those strings should be unaffected by running the macro, regardless of the order in which they appear.

How is it possible that the macro will fail to switch two different strings regardless of their original order?

9.2.2 Solution

The key is the statement that compares two strings:

```
%if &&word&j < &&word&i %then %do;
```

When the %IF comparison contains an arithmetic operator, macro language automatically applies the %EVAL function. So here are two sets of strings that will remain in their original order:

```
%let list = 3-3 0 5/8 1-1/1;
%let list = 5/8 1-1/1 3-3 0;
```

The %IF comparison finds equalities every time, never an inequality.

In the classroom, math ranges from simple arithmetic to differential equations and more. You have to pick the level of knowledge that is right for you. Macro language arithmetic similarly can involve more than one level of knowledge.

Part 3: Execution

Preparation ... learning about a wide range of tools ... is essential. Practice ... experimenting with these tools and pushing their limits ... is vital. But there is more to developing easy-to-use macros that accomplish sophisticated tasks. Experience ... developing a style and a comfort level with the techniques ... frees your mind and lets you envision the possibilities. That's what lets you invent macros that look like magic. This section presents some techniques, macros, and approaches to help in taking that final step.

Chapter 10: Generating Text

When macro language generates a word, the software figures out what to do with that word. The software might incorporate the word into a macro language statement, or it might embed the word as part of a SAS language statement. While that sounds simple, it leads to some interesting coding techniques.

10.1 Utilizing Generated Text

Here is some legitimate code that could appear within a macro definition:

```
data    %do quarter=1 %to 4;
             q&quarter
        %end;
        ;
```

Each word, whether hard-coded or generated by macro language, gets incorporated into the SAS program, producing:

```
data q1 q2 q3 q4;
```

Notice how:

- A macro variable can resolve into as little as part of a word within a SAS program.
- Multiple semicolons might seem confusing, but there is a trick to interpreting them. Match each semicolon to the macro language statement that it completes. Any remaining semicolons become generated text.

Next, reconsider the %BUBBLY macro from Chapter 9. The essence of the code was this:

```
%macro bubbly (macvar);
   %** Code to break up &macvar into 4 words,    ;
   %** then reorder the words.                   ;
   %let &macvar=&word1 &word2 &word3 &word4;
%mend bubbly;
```

As originally written, this macro replaces the incoming macro variable with the same words but in a different order. But what if the objective were slightly different, such as:

- Write the reordered words with a %PUT statement.
- Assign the reordered words to a different macro variable instead of replacing the original.

To add this sort of flexibility, a cumbersome approach would add parameters to the macro definition:

- A yes/no parameter to control whether a %PUT statement should write the reordered words.
- The name of another macro variable that should hold the reordered words. (If this parameter is left blank, replace the original incoming macro variable.)

Even with these added complexities, the macro might require modification down the road if additional objectives were added. A better approach would simplify the macro by changing the last line:

```
%macro bubbly (macvar);
   %** Code to break up &macvar into 4 words,    ;
   %** then reorder the words                    ;
   &word1 &word2 &word3 &word4
%mend bubbly;
```

This version looks strange. It dumps four words into the middle of a program. Oddly enough, this approach adds the flexibility needed to accomplish any of the objectives. For example, this macro call replaces &LIST with four words in a new order:

```
%let list = %bubbly (list);
```

When the macro executes, it generates four words in a new order, producing:

```
%let list = &word1 &word2 &word3 &word4;
```

Similarly, this statement assigns those four words as the value of a new macro variable:

```
%let new_macro_variable = %bubbly (list);
```

And this statement writes the four words in their new order:

```
%put %bubbly (list);
```

This statement puts the four reordered words into a DATA step array:

```
array _4_words {4} %bubbly (list);
```

In every case, executing the macro generates four words as text. The four words get added to the middle of a program, completing either a macro language statement or a SAS language statement. It is not necessary for the macro to define how those four words are going to be used.

Generating text broadens a macro's applicability, without adding parameters to its definition. Let's examine a few useful examples.

10.2 Counting Words in a String

When a macro parameter contains a series of variable names, it helps to know how many names are in the list. Clearly, macro language can count them:

```
%macro countem (list_of_words);
    %local i;
    %let i=0;
    %if %length(&list_of_words) %then
    %do %until (%scan(&list_of_words, &i+1, %str( )) = );
        %let i=%eval(&i + 1);
    %end;
%mend countem;
```

The %STR function defines blanks as the only possible delimiter for the %SCAN function. Because most lists in SAS programs are lists of variables or data sets, other delimiters would hardly ever be needed. When this macro runs, the final value of &I is the number of words encountered. But a %LOCAL variable won't be useful once the macro finishes executing. How can the program utilize the final value of &I? The best way is to generate it as text. Add one more line to the macro definition, just before the %MEND statement:

```
%macro countem (list_of_words);
    %local i;
    %let i=0;
    %if %length(&list_of_words) %then
    %do %until (%scan(&list_of_words, &i+1, %str( )) = );
        %let i=%eval(&i + 1);
    %end;
    &i
%mend countem;
```

Once the final &I resolves into text, that text gets added to the program as part of a macro statement or as part of a SAS language statement. All of these statements could utilize that generated text:

```
%let n_words = %countem (&var_list);
array vars {%countem (&var_list)} &var_list;
%do i=1 %to %countem (&var_list);
```

Other methods exist to count words. For example, this DATA step formula works in most cases:

```
if string=' ' then n_words=0;
else n_words = 1 + length(compbl(string)) - length(compress(string));
```

The COMPBL function replaces multiple, consecutive blanks with a single blank. The COMPRESS function removes all blanks. Macro language can utilize these functions by applying %SYSFUNC:

```
%if %length(&string)=0 %then %let n_words=0;
%else %let n_words = %eval( 1 + %length(%sysfunc(compbl(&string))) -
                           %length(%sysfunc(compress(&string))));
```

In practice, this formula usually works. However, it over counts by 1 if the incoming string contains any leading blanks. Left-hand-justifying the incoming string is safer (although it adds to the complexity of the code).

Advances in the software have actually made this macro obsolete. This expression counts the number of words in a string, without defining a macro:

```
%sysfunc(countw(&string, %str( )))
```

SAS language uses COUNTW to count the number of words in a string, and %SYSFUNC allows macro language to invoke the SAS language function. It should be noted that earlier releases of the software can encounter trouble with this syntax when &STRING is null. To counteract that, it can be helpful to add %SUPERQ:

```
%sysfunc(countw(%superq(string), %str( )))
```

Let's move on to another example of generating text.

10.3 Working with Lists

Once again, a macro parameter contains a list of variable names. When the list is long (or perhaps when concatenating two or more lists), it might be burdensome for the user to check that there are no duplicates on the list. So a macro is designed to remove duplicate words from the list:

```
%macro dedup (word_list);
    %local i next_word deduped_list;
    %if %length(&word_list) %then
    %do i=1 %to %sysfunc(countw(&word_list, %str( )));
        %let next_word = %scan(&word_list, &i, %str( ));
        %if %index(%str( &deduped_list ), %str( &next_word ))=0
        %then %let deduped_list = &deduped_list &next_word;
    %end;
%mend dedup;
```

The macro examines every word in the incoming list. Any word that has not been found before gets added to &DEDUPED_LIST. The %STR function adds leading and trailing blanks within the %INDEX function. That's necessary because the %INDEX function searches for strings, not words. Without those extra blanks, the %INDEX function would, for example, never add var1 to a list that already contains var10.

While the final value of &DEDUPED_LIST contains the proper list of words, the macro still has to make that final list available to the program. Once again, the best solution is to generate that list as text:

```
%macro dedup (word_list);
    %local i next_word deduped_list;
    %if %length(&word_list) %then
    %do i=1 %to %sysfunc(countw(&word_list, %str( )));
        %let next_word = %scan(&word_list, &i, %str( ));
        %if %index(%str( &deduped_list ), %str( &next_word ))=0
        %then %let deduped_list = &deduped_list &next_word;
    %end;
    &deduped_list
%mend dedup;
```

Generating text as the output increases flexibility without adding complexity. Two sample applications:

```
%let var_list = %dedup(&var_list);
%do i=1 %to %sysfunc(countw(%dedup(&list1 &list2 &list3), %str( )));
```

In its current form, %DEDUP treats var1 and VAR1 as two different words. Yet most applications will involve lists of variable names or data set names, where capitalization should not matter. The macro would be more valuable with a second parameter:

```
%macro dedup (word_list, case_matters=N);
```

If programming standards permit changing user-entered parameters, a one-line addition would satisfy the requirements:

```
%if &case_matters=N %then %let word_list = %upcase(&word_list);
```

The rest of the macro would remain unchanged. However, if programming standards discourage changing a user-entered parameter, a more complex enhancement would be needed. The macro could apply the existing logic when &case_matters=Y but would otherwise use:

```
%if &case_matters=N %then %do;
    %if %index(%str( %upcase(&deduped_list) ),
             %str( %upcase(&next_word) ))=0
    %then %let deduped_list = &deduped_list &next_word;
%end;
```

Perhaps a simpler alternative would process a new macro variable:

```
%let new_macro_variable = %upcase(&word_list);
```

In any event, similar macros could combine the same tools in slightly different ways to generate a variety of results:

- Find (and return) the overlap between two lists.
- Verify that every word in one list also appears in another list.

For example, this macro returns the overlapping words that appear in both of two lists:

```
%macro overlap (list1=, list2=);
    %local i next_word overlapping_words;
    %if %length(&list1) %then
    %do i=1 %to %sysfunc(countw(&list1, %str( )));
        %let next_word = %scan(&list1, &i, %str( ));
        %if %index(%str( &list2 ), %str( &next_word )) %then
        %let overlapping_words = &overlapping_words &next_word;
    %end;
    &overlapping_words
%mend overlap;
```

In its current form, the macro accumulates overlapping words into a macro variable (&OVERLAPPING_WORDS) and then generates the final list as text. However, for this purpose, it would be simpler to generate each word separately, without accumulating the overlapping words into a list:

```
%macro overlap (list1=, list2=);
    %local i next_word;
    %if %length(&list1) %then %do i=1 %to %countem(&list1);
        %let next_word = %scan(&list1, &i, %str( ));
```

```
        %if %index(%str( &list2 ), %str( &next_word )) %then
        &next_word;
    %end;
%mend overlap;
```

For this particular application, macro language can generate text one word at a time.

10.4 Prefer the Macro Solution

SAS often provides many feasible approaches to a programming problem. If the choices include a 100% macro-based approach, there may be text-generating advantages. Consider this example, where the objective is to capture the number of observations in a SAS data set. Here is a simple approach:

```
data _null_;
    call symputx('n_obs', how_many);
    stop;
    set incoming.dataset nobs=how_many;
run;
```

Note these features:

- Macro language performs very little of the work.

- The SET statement option NOBS= creates HOW_MANY during the compilation phase of the DATA step. CALL SYMPUT can retrieve that value as soon as the execution phase begins.

- Theoretically, the result could be incorrect. The observation count includes observations that have been marked for deletion, but have not yet been physically removed from the data set.

A different approach can account for the deleted observations:

```
proc sql noprint;
    select nobs - delobs into : n_obs
            from dictionary.tables
            where libname='INCOMING' and memname='DATASET';
quit;
```

PROC SQL can access both necessary pieces of information: the total number of observations (NOBS) and the number of deleted observations (DELOBS).

A purely macro-based approach, while more complex, can also account for deleted observations:

```
%let dsn_id = %sysfunc(open(incoming.dataset));
%let n_obs = %sysfunc(attrn(&dsn_id, nlobs));
%let dsn_id = %sysfunc(close(&dsn_id));
```

The data set attribute NLOBS is the number of "logical" observations: the total number that exist minus those that have been marked for deletion.

Any of these programming approaches could be encapsulated in a macro. Using the first approach, the macro would become:

```
%macro how_many_obs (dsn);
   %global n_obs;
   data _null_;
      call symputx('n_obs', how_many);
      stop;
      set &dsn nobs=how_many;
   run;
%mend how_many_obs;
```

However, only the purely macro-based solution can successfully generate text as the outcome:

```
%macro pure_macro_based_solution (dsn);
   %local dsn_id n_obs;
   %let dsn_id = %sysfunc(open(&dsn));
   %let n_obs = %sysfunc(attrn(&dsn_id, nlobs));
   %let dsn_id = %sysfunc(close(&dsn_id));
   &n_obs
%mend pure_macro_based_solution;
```

All of these statements can make use of the generated text:

```
%let any_var_i_choose = %pure_macro_based_solution (incoming.dataset);
%if %pure_macro_based_solution (incoming.dataset) > 2000 %then %do;
do i=1 to %pure_macro_based_solution (incoming.dataset);
```

However, other approaches fail when encapsulated as a text-generating macro. This variation tries to generate text with the DATA step approach:

```
%macro how_many_obs (dsn);
   data _null_;
      call symputx('n_obs', how_many);
      stop;
      set &dsn nobs=how_many;
   run;
   &n_obs
%mend how_many_obs;
%let any_var_i_choose = %how_many_obs (incoming.dataset);
```

This generates a strange, non-working result:

```
%let any_var_i_choose = data _null_;
call symputx('n_obs', how_many);
stop;
set &dsn nobs=how_many;
run;
&n_obs
```

After assigning an unusual value for &ANY_VAR_I_CHOOSE, the program then generates three DATA step statements that appear outside of a DATA step. Clearly, these statements won't do the job. Only the pure macro solution generates text in a useful, flexible fashion.

Even when text generation is not a requirement, a pure macro-based approach has advantages. Consider this scenario:

- %A constructs the beginning of a DATA step.
- %B constructs the middle of that DATA step.
- %C constructs the ending of that DATA step.

Under these circumstances, any of these macros could invoke the pure macro version of %HOW_MANY_OBS. But any definition of %HOW_MANY_OBS that includes SAS language statements would fail. For example, think about the result if %B were to invoke a version of %HOW_MANY_OBS that generates SAS language statements. Those SAS language statements would unfortunately be inserted into the DATA step that begins with %A and ends with %C.

Chapter 11: Debugging

By nature, debugging macros is more difficult than debugging SAS programs. The major confounding factors are:

- Errors might stem from either macro language or from the generated SAS code.

- The line number references on macro error messages indicate which macro is causing the problem but not which line within the macro.

This chapter assumes familiarity with standard options such as MPRINT, SYMBOLGEN, and MLOGIC. In fact, Section 4.5 showed how to capture the current settings for these options, temporarily override them, and restore them to their original values at a later point. Current releases of the software have added more options, including:

- MPRINTNEST and MLOGICNEST, which display the names of all currently executing macros (in nested order) rather than just the innermost executing macro.

- MAUTOLOCDISPLAY, which displays the source of a macro when invoking it through the autocall facility.

The focus here, however, is on programming magic rather than switching an option on or off. For example, how can a program:

- Store the generated SAS code in a separate file, so that the file can be run as a SAS program devoid of macro language?

- Use a macro parameter to control whether or not diagnostic steps (such as running a PROC CONTENTS, printing 10 observations of a data set, or writing the values of macro variables) should execute?

- End a program as soon as an error is encountered, along with generating a message about which DATA or PROC step contained the error?

Each of the next three sections addresses one of these topics.

11.1 Store the Generated SAS Code

When macro language error messages become difficult to interpret, store the macro-generated SAS statements in a separate file. The generated file may contain some obvious problems. But if not, run that file without any reference to macro language. The error messages should be easier to interpret.

It takes just two small steps to store the generated SAS statements. First, define a file using the keyword MPRINT as the FILENAME:

```
filename mprint 'path_to_some_file';
```

And, second, turn on the proper options:

```
options mfile mprint;
```

That's all it takes! Running the program will now save the macro-generated SAS statements in the designated file. The spacing and indentation may not adhere to your usual high standards, but the statements will be captured and available to run again without interference from the macro facility.

The techniques from Section 4.2 can embellish these results in several ways. To begin, direct the generated source code to follow the location of the program:

```
filename mprint "%sysfunc(getoption(sysin))code";
options mfile mprint;
```

This combination directs the generated source code; when running prog1.sas, the code automatically gets saved as prog1.sascode.

What if the program runs several macros sequentially, generating thousands of lines of source code? It might be convenient to split up those lines into manageable sections. For example, if prog1.sas runs %MACRO1, then %MACRO2, and then %MACRO3, it might be convenient to save the generated source code as prog1.macro1, prog1.macro2, and prog1.macro3. Just a small amount of preparation can make this happen. First, retrieve the path to the program:

```
%let program_path = %sysfunc(getoption(sysin));
%let program_path = %substr(&program_path,1,%length(&program_path)-3);
```

At this point, &PROGRAM_PATH is the complete path to the program, minus the letters sas at the end.

Then modify the definition of %MACRO1, %MACRO2, and %MACRO3 by adding three lines to each:

```
filename mprint clear;
filename mprint "&program_path.&sysmacroname";
options mfile mprint;
```

The automatic variable &SYSMACRONAME contains the name of the currently executing macro.

11.2 Control Diagnostic Messages

When macros defy debugging, add diagnostic steps to the macro. %PUT statements display the values of macro variables and indicate whether a certain portion of the macro is executing. Investigate the data more carefully by adding a PROC CONTENTS here and there, along with a PROC PRINT of the first 10 observations of a SAS data set. Add a few more variables to the TABLES statement in PROC FREQ or the VAR statement in PROC MEANS. In short, modify the macro to provide more information that will help diagnose the problem.

Of course, once the problem has been found and corrected, all those diagnostic steps will need to be removed from the macro … or will they? Try a different approach. Write the macro with a parameter that controls whether the diagnostic steps run or not. Turn the diagnostic steps on when debugging is needed, but leave them off otherwise.

Here is a simple approach:

```
%macro whatever (debug=N,  . . .  more parameters);
```

&DEBUG controls whether or not the diagnostic steps should run. Within the macro, any of these additions could execute:

```
%if &debug=Y %then %do;
    proc print data=people (obs=10);
    run;
    proc contents data=people;
    run;
%end;

proc means data=people;
   var salary age
       %if &debug=Y %then tax_bracket bonus;
       ;
run;

%if &debug=Y %then %put _user_;
```

Plan ahead by adding this extra parameter and anticipating which diagnostics would help. But remember, if the existing diagnostics don't resolve the problem, it is always possible to add more … just keep their execution dependent upon &DEBUG.

11.3 End When the Error Occurs

Wouldn't it be nice if a program would just end when an error occurs? Don't execute any more DATA or PROC steps, don't clutter up the log with messages about steps that got skipped, and don't even execute any more macro language statements. Just halt. And as an added bonus, issue a message about which macro-generated DATA or PROC step is causing the error condition. Macro language can make this happen!

This section explores a variety of tools to consider. Along the way, you may notice that there is more than one "right" way to use these tools. Consider that:

- Some tools require more effort than others.
- It would be inconvenient to halt SAS entirely, if you are in the middle of an interactive session.
- Warning messages may halt a program. Should halting require an error condition instead?

Let's begin the discussion with an easy-to-use tool, the automatic macro variable &SYSERR. Every DATA and PROC step resets the value of &SYSERR, using this scheme of values:

- 0 = 100% successful execution (neither errors nor warnings)
- 1, 2, 5, 6 = the user took an action that cancelled the DATA or PROC step
- 3 = SAS entered syntax-checking mode
- 4 = the step generated a warning

Values greater than 6 indicate that the step contains some sort of error condition. The simplest application of &SYSERR requires 100% successful execution for a program to continue. Here is a simple example. Compare these two versions of a macro:

```
%macro run_many;              %macro run_many;
   %macro1                        %macro1
   %macro2                        %if &syserr=0 %then %macro2;
   %macro3                        %if &syserr=0 %then %macro3;
%mend run_many;               %mend run_many;
```

The first version always attempts to run all three macros. The second version will run a macro only when there are no errors or warnings in the final step of the prior macro.

The subject of warning messages is a tricky one. It is possible for a macro to generate a series of DATA and PROC steps where one of them along the way generates a warning. The value of &SYSERR can get set to 4 by one DATA or PROC step and then reset to 0 by a later step. So the program on the right might run %MACRO2, even though there is an earlier warning message. Later on, this chapter will construct a convenient way to examine &SYSERR for every single DATA and PROC step individually. An alternative would be to switch from &SYSERR to &SYSCC, which does not get reset to 0 by a successful DATA or PROC step.

Finally, if warning messages are acceptable, this logic might be an improvement:

```
%if &syserr=0 or &syserr=4 %then %do;
```

Beginning with SAS 9.2, macro language supports the IN operator (as long as the MINOPERATOR option has been turned on):

```
%if &syserr in (0 4) %then %do;
```

Be sure to check both the syntax and related options when using the IN operator. To make things simple (and to accommodate the author's preference as well), the remaining examples all assume there should be no errors and no warnings.

Halting a program is relatively easy. Here is one way (macro language also contains an %ABORT statement):

```
%if &syserr > 0 %then %do;
    %put Now halting the program.;
    endsas;
%end;
```

The ENDSAS statement halts the entire program. If you are using interactive SAS, it will shut down SAS entirely. For cases when that is undesirable, this section will explore an alternative approach shortly.

What would it take to halt a program as soon as an error or warning appears? Is it really feasible to add this sort of checking after every DATA and PROC step? Wouldn't that require enclosing code in a macro, due to the %IF %THEN statements? The combined answer to all these questions is a short macro:

```
%macro runn (message);
    run;
    %if &syserr > 0 %then %do;
        %put Now halting the program.;
        %put Location:  &message;
        endsas;
    %end;
%mend runn;
```

Programs would call this macro instead of using RUN statements:

```
proc means data=sales;
   var amount tax;
   class state;
%runn (proc means just after the giant merge step)
```

The macro adds the RUN statement, causing PROC MEANS to run. It checks &SYSERR to determine if there was any sort of error or warning. If so, it generates a message and halts the program. And all these changes just involve replacing the RUN statement with a %RUNN statement. Even the message is optional. A null message will cause no harm. However, be sure to add parentheses for a null message:

```
%runn ( )
```

Otherwise the macro will wait to execute. In fact, an interactive session will just hang, never running the final DATA or PROC step. Why? Interactively, the programmer could submit this much:

```
%runn
```

Then the programmer could submit the rest:

```
(proc means just after the giant merge step)
```

Without the parentheses, the next batch of submitted code could, in theory, be supplying a value for &MESSAGE. So the program waits …

Speaking of interactive sessions, it would be inconvenient to have SAS shut down because of an error or warning. The log would disappear, making debugging impossible. To work around this issue, consider the following program:

```
proc means data=sales;
   var amount tax;
   class state;
run cancel;
```

The word "cancel" tells SAS to skip running PROC MEANS. The idea, once a program encounters an error or warning, now becomes:

- Continue executing the program, but
- Change all RUN statements to RUN CANCEL statements.

Subsequent DATA and PROC steps may add to the log, but they will not run. The last step that actually runs is the one generating the error.

Just a few changes to %RUNN will make this happen:

```
%macro runn (message);
   %global _cancel_;
   run &_cancel_;
   %if &syserr > 0 %then %do;
      %put *** Here is the PROBLEM ***;
      %put Location:  &message;
      %let _cancel_=cancel;
   %end;
%mend runn;
```

This variation nearly works, but it contains a somewhat hidden drawback. When the RUN CANCEL statement executes, SAS considers that the user has cancelled the step. The value of &SYSERR is set to 1, not 0. While all subsequent DATA and PROC steps will not run, every subsequent %RUNN will generate another message about where the problem lies. To correct that, make a slight change:

```
%macro runn (message);
   %global _cancel_;
   run &_cancel_;
   %if &syserr > 1 %then %do;
      %put *** Here is the PROBLEM ***;
      %put Macro:  &sysmacroname;
      %put Location:  &message;
      %let _cancel_=cancel;
   %end;
   options nosource nonotes;
%mend runn;
```

Finally, what would happen if you are late paying the bill for your software license renewal? Programs start generating warning messages when the software license is close to expiring. Would these warnings affect &SYSERR and cause your programs to terminate early? No. It turns out that these warnings have no impact on &SYSERR (at least for current releases of the software). Just to be safe, when many programs contain many %RUNN statements, there should be a way to turn them back into RUN; statements. Of course, complex approaches exist where a new global macro variable could control how %RUNN operates. But the simplest way requires adding three lines to the beginning of a program:

```
%macro runn;
   run;
%mend runn;
```

By defining %RUNN within the program, the program never needs to search the autocall library. Instead, it executes the already defined version wherever %RUNN appears.

Chapter 12: Complexity vs. Simplicity

Simplicity has obvious advantages. It makes macros easier to write, understand, and maintain. When is complexity the right path? Many legitimate answers exist, such as:

- When the end users are not so sophisticated and require the macros to do more of the work. Chapter 11 illustrated how to end a program when an error condition occurs, while providing a useful message. This chapter will explore additional topics, such as checking the macro parameters before starting to execute.

- When the macro must adapt to many environments, such as across multiple operating systems or both batch and interactive applications.

- When added complexity generates a faster running program or a more capable macro.

Before tackling the serious answers, let's briefly explore the wrong answer.

12.1 Building Job Security

Complex macros fortify job security. But building complexity into a macro just for the sake of job security is another matter. Unfortunately, for a handful of programmers, this is not just a goal but an art form. After all, why code a simple statement like this?

```
%let lullaby = 1;
```

Wouldn't this logic be much more elegant?

```
%let lullaby = %eval(no ne na);
```

Because "no" is not equal to "na", the comparison is true and %EVAL returns a 1. (For similar %EVAL examples, refer to Section 9.2.) If that is too easy, try "enhancing" this overly simple statement:

```
%let pi = 3.14;
```

Remember, %SYSEVALF performs non-integer arithmetic:

```
%let pi = %sysevalf(0.11+3.03**(y=%substr(&sysday, %length(&sysday))));
```

Of course, &SYSDAY contains the current day of the week, and every day of the week ends in "y". So the y= comparison inside %SYSEVALF is always true and the partially evaluated statement resolves into:

```
%let pi = %sysevalf(0.11 + 3.03**1);
```

Naturally, expressly coding the %EVAL or %SYSEVALF function might be too big a clue. Another programmer might actually be able to decipher your code. Why not use comparisons in places where the software automatically invokes %EVAL for you? Consider this all-too-simple %DO loop:

```
%do i=1 %to 5;
```

Anyone can follow that. Try replacing it with this beauty:

```
%do i = no ne na %to (Ep Eq Ep) + 4;
```

Remember, %DO loops automatically invoke %EVAL for the FROM, TO, and BY values. Because Ep is equal to Ep, the partially resolved statement becomes:

```
%do i = 1 %to (1) + 4;
```

Use %EVAL to disguise the fact that sections of your macro do nothing. Here is a stripped-down example:

```
%macro disguise (indata=, top=8, middle=5, bottom=2);
    %if &top > &middle > &bottom %then %do;
        proc princess data=&indata;
            var _numeric_;
            output out=kingdoms;
        run;
    %end;
%mend disguise;
```

Of course, there is no such thing as PROC PRINCESS. But if you saw this code buried inside a working macro, would you try to track it down? The key is understanding the %IF comparison:

```
8 > 5 > 2
```

A DATA step evaluates this as two conditions:

```
(8 > 5) and (5 > 2)
```

Both comparisons are true, and the DATA step interprets the entire expression as being true. However, macro language evaluates the %IF conditions from left to right:

```
(8 > 5) > 2
```

%EVAL finds that 8 is greater than 5 and replaces the true comparison with a 1:

```
(1) > 2
```

%EVAL finds this comparison is false, so the macro never generates PROC PRINCESS. Are you feeling more secure yet?

Finally, why should another programmer be allowed to use your macros without asking you for instructions? Construct default parameters that must be blanked out for the macro to work. For example:

```
%macro mine_not_yours (p1=OB, p2=L_B, p3=CAL);
   data new;
      set old (&p3&p2&p1);
   run;
%mend mine_not_yours;
```

Anyone who dares to use this macro while leaving the default parameters in place will receive a message:

```
Invalid option name CALL_BOB.
```

Of course, you can adjust the message to be nicer or nastier. Are you inspired yet? Try this small test before moving on.

12.1.1 Programming Challenge #8

The sample statements below generate 0 or 1 as their result.

```
%let eq1 = %eval(eq);              → 1
%let eq2 = %eval(eq eq);           → 0
%let eq3 = %eval(eq eq eq);        → 0
%let eq4 = %eval(eq eq eq eq);     → 0
%let eq5 = %eval(eq eq eq eq eq);  → 0
```

Why are these the results?

12.1.2 Solution

If the series were extended, all the additional statements would generate 0. To understand why, apply three resolution rules:

- In every case, EQ is a comparison operator.
- %EVAL replaces true comparisons with a 1 and false comparisons with a 0.
- Multiple comparisons evaluate from left to right.

Consider the first and third statements. The first statement compares a null value to a null value. Because they are equal, %EVAL returns a 1. The third statement begins the same way, starting with the leftmost comparison. The partially resolved statement becomes:

```
%let eq3 = %eval(1 eq eq);
```

The next EQ comparison compares 1 to a null value. Because they are not equal, %EVAL returns a 0. So the partially resolved statement now becomes:

```
%let eq3 = %eval(0 eq);
```

Finally, the last EQ comparison compares 0 to a null value. Because they are not equal, %EVAL returns its final value, 0. Based on these results, impress your colleagues by explaining what will work and what will fail in this statement:

```
%do i=ga ge go %to na ne no %by eq eq eq;
```

Assuming that job security does not justify added complexity, what are the valid reasons? The remainder of this chapter explores those situations.

12.2 Ease of Use

Remember that despite their flaws, end users play a vital role in the life of programmers. Make their life as easy as possible! Take on more of the burden when writing a macro if it will make life easier for those who use the macro.

Let's begin with a simple example. Consider a macro that compares a SAS log with a SAS program. It must determine whether there is a match: did the current version of the program generate the log? The details of such a macro, including its feasibility and limitations, lie beyond the scope of this book. Our only concern here is ease of use. The macro call would look like this:

```
%compare (program_name=/path/to/folder/some_program.sas,
          log_name=/path/to/folder/some_program.log)
```

For the vast majority of calls to %COMPARE, the names of the program and log will match except for the last three letters. The simpler implementation would force the user to enter both parameters, increasing both the burden and the chance for a typographical error. The more complex (for the programmer) implementation would allow one parameter to remain blank. In that case, the macro would derive the value for the other parameter.

How much extra complexity would be involved? The macro might begin by checking whether &LOG_NAME is blank. This would be the wrong way:

```
%if &log_name= %then %do;
```

This statement runs into trouble when the user-entered &LOG_NAME contains either a forward slash or a dash. Depending on the operating system, those characters could be legitimate parts of a filename. However, they also constitute arithmetic operators. As explained in Chapter 9, the %IF condition triggers the %EVAL function, where the combination of arithmetic operators and letters would generate an error. This variation easily overcomes the problem:

```
%if %length(&log_name)=0 %then %do;
```

That's the safer way to check for a null value.

Next, the macro would have to construct the matching name to assign &LOG_NAME. These assumptions (while not appropriate for every operating system) would make the task easy:

- The name of the program ends with .sas
- The name of the log ends with .log

In that case, one statement would do the trick:

```
%let log_name = %substr(&program_name, 1, %length(&program_name)-3)log;
```

What should happen if the name of the incoming program does not end with .sas? Those complications are beyond the scope of this book. However, note that macro language can easily verify whether that assumption is true:

```
%local suffix;
%let suffix = %scan(&program_name, -1, .);
%if %qupcase(&suffix)=SAS %then %do;
```

As noted in Section 2.1, the %SCAN function reads from right to left when the second parameter is negative. While the %UPCASE function would uppercase its argument, the %QUPCASE function also quotes the result. That would be necessary if it turns out that the last portion of the program name was not "sas" but was "and" or "or". Without some sort of quoting function, these statements would be trouble:

```
%if AND=SAS %then %do;
%if OR=SAS %then %do;
```

But the real lesson here is not the syntax. The real lesson is to shift the work from the user to the macro. The additional programming complexity lets the user leave the second parameter blank most of the time.

Consider another example, where our unsophisticated users apply a macro to subset and analyze data. The generated SAS code might look like this:

```
proc means data=huge.database;
    var salary bonus;
    where zipcode="01801";
    title "Salaries for Zipcode 01801";
run;
```

The user merely has to specify:

```
%analyze (zipcode=01801)
```

But one day a user gets creative:

```
%analyze (zipcode=parents_zipcode)
```

Reasonably or not, the user wants to analyze salaries where children live in the same ZIP code as their parents. Of course, that macro won't work. The generated code looks like this:

```
proc means data=huge.database;
    var salary bonus;
    where zipcode="parents_zipcode";
    title "Salaries for Zipcode parents_zipcode";
run;
```

The WHERE clause selects zero observations. But why shouldn't the macro work? If the macro could determine that the user has passed a variable name instead of a variable value, the generated code would have to change just a bit:

```
proc means data=huge.database;
    var salary bonus;
    where zipcode=parents_zipcode;
    title "Salaries for Zipcode equal to parents_zipcode";
run;
```

To make this happen, the program has to determine that, in this case, the user entered a variable name. The software provides many tools to check for that. The COMPRESS function can remove all digits by specifying "d" as the third parameter:

```
%if %length(%sysfunc(compress(&zipcode,,d))=0 %then %do;
```

Or the ANYALPHA function can determine whether a value contains any letters:

```
%if %sysfunc(anyalpha(&zipcode)) %then %do;
```

Without delving into the details of the final macro structure, the lesson resonates clearly. When possible, shift the work from the user to the macro. And remember, most unreasonable requests on the part of users reflect an analytical need.

12.3 Checking Parameters

How much checking should a macro perform on values the user has entered? Some macros double their length by checking before executing. Even in simple cases, apply some judgment. If the user is supposed to enter Y or N for a parameter, which of these alternatives are acceptable?

```
get_reports=Y
get_reports=YES
get_reports=y
get_reports=yes
get_reports=YeS
get_reports=Yoyo
```

There are no clear cut right and wrong answers to this question. It is reasonable to accept any form of Y or YES and any form of N or NO. It is equally reasonable to accept Y or N, but nothing else. It is up to the programmer to draw the line, to determine how easy the user's life should be. Whatever your decision, it will affect the complexity of your macro.

How much checking makes sense? Has the user entered a value for all required parameters? Are user-entered values legal? Do combinations of user-entered parameters make sense? Consider specific user-entered values:

- Does a folder exist?
- Does a file exist?
- Does a SAS data set exist?
- Does a list of variables exist within a SAS data set?

Functions can answer all these questions. For example, the FEXIST and FILEEXIST functions check for the existence of a file or a folder. FILEEXIST expects the full path, while FEXIST expects the filename:

```
filename fname "path to some file or folder";
%let results = %sysfunc(fexist(fname));
```

These statements assign &RESULTS a value of 1 when the file exists and 0 when it does not. Notice that the program can detect an error condition without necessarily assigning the result to a macro variable. The following %DO group executes when the file or folder does not exist:

```
%if not %sysfunc(fexist(fname)) %then %do;
```

Checking for the existence of a SAS data set is just as easy. Again, the %DO group executes when the SAS data set does not exist:

```
%if not %sysfunc(exist(mylib.my_dataset)) %then %do;
```

Additional parameters extend the capability of the EXIST function. It can detect more complex conditions, such as whether or not a catalog exists. However, those features are not needed to check parameters that a user would typically enter.

Checking for the existence of a variable is a little bit trickier. The three-step process involves:

1. Open the data set that should contain the variable.
2. Attempt to locate the variable within the data set.
3. Close the data set.

Each statement below accomplishes one of these three steps:

```
%let dataset_id = %sysfunc(open(mylib.my_dataset),i);
%let var_found  = %sysfunc(varnum(&dataset_id,variable_name));
%let dataset_id = %sysfunc(close(&dataset_id));
```

Here are some key points:

- The first statement opens the incoming data set and assigns an integer value to &DATASET_ID. The value of the integer is actually a sequential count of the data sets that have been opened so far. However, the value is not important. What is important is that the assigned number can now be used by later functions to identify the data set.

- The second statement searches the data set for the target variable VARIABLE_NAME. It extracts the variable number within the data set and assigns that number to &VAR_FOUND. If VARIABLE_NAME cannot be found, &VAR_FOUND receives a value of 0.

- The third statement closes the data set.

Following these three statements, macro language can examine the value of &VAR_FOUND to ensure that it is greater than 0.

Why jump through these hoops when SAS has other ways to determine whether or not a variable exists? For example, PROC SQL can retrieve information about any existing variable (using DICTIONARY.COLUMNS) and any existing data set (using DICTIONARY.TABLES). There is a good reason to add the complexity, however. Macro language statements have an advantage over other approaches, such as PROC SQL. Macro language statements can execute at the beginning of a macro, even when that macro builds just the middle section of a DATA step. Refer to similar examples in Section 10.4, "Prefer the Macro Solution."

Some applications require unusual critical conditions. For example:

- Does a CLASS variable ever take on a missing value?

Think through the possibilities for both conditions in the data and the objectives of the users. How sophisticated are the end users? What is the cost if a macro fails? But draw the line at some point, and rely on the user to enter intelligent values. The end product is a macro, not an off-the-shelf software package. Expect that an application will occasionally require debugging.

12.4 Portability

Programmers rarely think about portability. Must a macro work on multiple operating systems? Must it work in both batch and interactive applications?

Section 4.2 illustrates how a macro can capture the name of a program and create an output file with a matching name. But what happens when the macro executes interactively, and there is no such thing as the name of the program?

This section will not solve all of those issues. The details are too intricate and too specific to a given application. Still, it is worth mentioning a few tools and how they might help:

- An automatic macro variable, &SYSPROCESSNAME, begins with the word "Program" for non-interactive programs.

- Another automatic variable, &SYSSCPL, returns the operating system. That information might be needed in order to execute a system command.

- Consider adding a parameter to name the output file for interactive applications but which can be left blank and calculated by non-interactive applications.

12.5 Complexity vs. Speed

Macros tend to get used repeatedly. When working with large data sets, this repetitive use brings efficiency into play. As an example, consider this program before encapsulating it into a macro:

```
proc summary data=my_data;
   var amount;
   output out=_statistics_ (keep=mean_value) mean=mean_value;
run;
data my_data;
   if _n_=1 then set _statistics_;
   set my_data;
   if amount > mean_value then amount_c='Greater';
   else if amount = mean_value then amount_c='Equal';
   else amount_c='Less';
   drop mean_value;
run;
```

The program compares AMOUNT to its mean value to assign AMOUNT_C. In macro form, the program might look like this:

```
%macro COMPARE (varname);
   proc summary data=my_data;
      var &varname;
      output out=_statistics_ (keep=mean_value) mean=mean_value;
   run;
   data my_data;
      if _n_=1 then set _statistics_;
      set my_data;
      if &varname > mean_value then &varname._c='Greater';
      else if &varname = mean_value then &varname._c='Equal';
      else &varname._c='Less';
      drop mean_value;
   run;
%mend COMPARE;
%COMPARE (amount)
```

In real life, the macro would set up parameters for the names of the input and output data sets. For this lesson, we can omit that. So where is the problem?

The day after the macro becomes available, an analyst calls the macro five times for the same data set:

```
%COMPARE (amount)
%COMPARE (salary)
%COMPARE (bonus)
%COMPARE (sales)
%COMPARE (profits)
```

Each macro call generates a PROC SUMMARY and a DATA step. To make matters worse, a junior programmer notices five macro calls and says, "Let me make your life easy. I'll write a macro you can call once instead of five times." The result:

```
%macro COMPARE2 (varlist);
    %local i next_varname;
    %do i=1 %to %sysfunc(countw(&varlist, %str( )));
        %let next_varname = %scan(&varlist, &i, %str( ));
        %COMPARE (&next_varname)
    %end;
%mend COMPARE2;
%COMPARE2 (amount salary bonus sales profits)
```

%COMPARE2 still generates five DATA and PROC steps, but now the problem is hidden. It's the job of the senior programmer to anticipate this situation, to talk with the users about how they will use the macro. The original %COMPARE macro should have been written differently, using a more complex logic to generate two steps instead of ten. The generated program could take this form:

```
proc summary data=my_data;
    var amount salary bonus sales profits;
    output out=_statistics_ (keep=mean_value_:)
           mean=mean_value_1 - mean_value_5;
run;
data my_data;
    if _n_=1 then set _statistics_;
    set my_data;
    if amount > mean_value_1 then amount_c='Greater';
    else if amount = mean_value_1 then amount_c='Equal';
    else amount_c='Less';
    if salary > mean_value_2 then salary_c='Greater';
    else if salary = mean_value_2 then salary_c='Equal';
    else salary_c='Less';
    if bonus > mean_value_3 then bonus_c='Greater';
    else if bonus = mean_value_3 then bonus_c='Equal';
    else bonus_c='Less';
    if sales > mean_value_4 then sales_c='Greater';
    else if sales = mean_value_4 then sales_c='Equal';
```

```
      else sales_c='Less';
      if profits > mean_value_5 then profits_c='Greater';
      else if profits = mean_value_5 then profits_c='Equal';
      else profits_c='Less';
      drop mean_value_:;
   run;
```

The macro that generates this code must be more complex, and it takes extra programming time to write. But it will run nearly five times faster. The new version might look like this:

```
%macro COMPARE (varlist);
   %local i next_varname n_varnames;
   %let n_varnames = %sysfunc(countw(&varlist, %str( )));
   proc summary data=my_data;
      var &varlist;
      output out=_statistics_ (keep=mean_value_:)
            mean=mean_value_1 - mean_value_&n_varnames;
   run;
   data my_data;
      if _n_=1 then set _statistics_;
      set my_data;
      %do i=1 %to &n_varnames;
         %let next_varname = %scan(&varlist, &i, %str( ));
         if &next_varname > mean_value_&i then
            &next_varname._c='Greater';
         else if &next_varname = mean_value_&i then
            &next_varname._c='Equal';
         else &next_varname._c='Less';
      %end;
      drop mean_value_:;
   run;
%mend COMPARE;
```

The extra programming time and complexity lets the new version of %COMPARE run faster and on a list of variables instead of a single variable.

12.6 Miscellaneous Applications

This section examines two more applications where added complexity eases the burden on the end user. The first program generates a monthly report, but it requires maintenance:

```
proc means data=sales;
   class region;
   var amount;
   title 'Sales for 2014-05';
   where ('01May2014'd <= sasdate <= '31May2014'd);
run;
```

This program runs monthly and requires that the three sections in **bold** change each month. But with a little ingenuity (and a little macro language), the changes can be automated. Consider this approach instead:

```
%let datevar = &sysdate9;

data _null_;
   call symputx('month_begin', intnx('month',"&datevar"d,-1));
   call symputx('month_end', intnx('month',"&datevar"d,0)-1);
   call symput('year_month',
               put(intnx('month',"&datevar"d,-1),yymmd7.));
run;
%put &month_begin;   → integer equivalent to 01May2014
%put &month_end;     → integer equivalent to 31May2014
%put &year_month;    → 2014-05
proc means data=sales;
   class region;
   var amount;
   title "Sales for &year_month";
   where (&month_begin <= sasdate <= &month_end);
run;
```

The key is that all three changes can be derived from the current date. The INTNX function returns the first day of a specified time period. Therefore:

- &MONTH_BEGIN is the first day of the month before the current date.
- &MONTH_END is the last day of the month before the current date.
- &YEAR_MONTH is the month before the current date, in YYYY-MM format.

No maintenance is required. Zero. All that is necessary is to run the program some time during the month in order to get the previous month's report. As an added bonus, the macro version will never make a mistake when computing the last day of the month.

Technically, there is no need to copy &SYSDATE9 into &DATEVAR. The program could have used &SYSDATE9 any place that &DATEVAR appears. However, creating &DATEVAR can simplify the process in another way. Consider overriding the %LET statement with:

```
%let datevar = 14Feb2014;
```

A change to &DATEVAR automatically passes through to all the other macro variables. If the report ever needs to be backdated, the changes are now limited to the single %LET statement at the top of the program instead of taking place at multiple points in the body of the program.

In the final example, end users are actually going to request the added functionality that they desire. A macro is supposed to be called with a list of variables to process:

```
%mymac (var_list = lastname firstname q1 q2 q3 q4)
```

Along comes an end user wanting to be able to pass variable lists, something like this parameter value:

```
%mymac (var_list = lastname n_: q1-q4)
```

How easy or difficult is it to allow that? Well, within limits, it's pretty simple. In many applications, the order of the variables doesn't matter and capitalization of variable names doesn't matter. In that case, PROC CONTENTS can parse the list and PROC SQL can capture all the individual variable names:

```
proc contents data=&in_data (keep=&var_list) noprint
   out=_contents_ (keep=name);
run;
proc sql noprint;
  select trim(name) into : var_list separated by ' '
  from _contents_;
quit;
```

Because the software already has the ability to parse variable lists, let the software transform the variable lists into a set of variable names! With very little added complexity, your macros can now parse variable lists. But is this good enough? What if the order of the variables is important? Does SAS possess a way to parse a list of variables, output the variable names, and maintain their order? PROC TRANSPOSE can do it:

```
proc transpose data=&in_data (obs=0) out=transposed (keep=_NAME_);
   var &var_list;
run;
proc sql noprint;
   select trim(_name_) into : var_list separated by ' '
   from transposed;
quit;
```

There is no need to actually transpose the data values. Transposing the variable names will be sufficient, hence OBS=0 on the PROC statement. But the transposed variable names will appear in order in the output data set, in _NAME_. All that is left to do is to retrieve the names.

Chapter 13: A Final Illusion: Backtesting

This chapter is an illusion, a vision of what could exist. Right now it exists only in the realm of imagination. Here is the situation that inspires this vision.

Many macros get updated from time to time. How do we know the new and old versions do substantially the same thing? Either formally or informally, we design a few tests, run them, and compare the results. What would happen a year later if someone suspected that the old version had not worked properly in all cases? It may be impossible to test. There may have been three or four updates in that period of time, and it may be impossible to recover the original version. Often, life goes on. We don't worry about what the old macro would have done, because the updated version is performing well. What if it becomes crucial to validate the original version of the macro … or perhaps to test the variation that existed at a particular point in time?

Now expand that thought to cover an entire library of macros. How can you run a program that calls eight macros, each of which calls two additional macros, and use the version of the macros that existed on a particular day six months ago? How do you prepare for the moment this is necessary, so that it becomes easy to do? This chapter covers the methods needed to turn this illusion into a reality, to easily store and access any version of any macro.

13.1 The Preparation

Macros within an autocall library typically contain a header block with information about the macro's purpose, author, inputs and outputs, history, and perhaps key usage notes. Consider this section from a header block:

```
%**                                                                **;
%**   Program Name:           /main/macro/library/my_macro.sas      **;
%**                                                                **;
%**   History/Modifications:                                       **;
%**            11/24/2012  Moved to main macro library             **;
%**            03/08/2013  Enhanced report 4 by switching from      **;
%**                        from proc print to proc report          **;
%**            07/03/2013  Added significance level parameter       **;
%**            10/15/2013  Added debugging tools                   **;
%**                                                                **;
```

At any point from November 24, 2012 onward, this macro resided in the main macro library under the name my_macro.sas. However, the contents of that file changed three times. Each time, the new version of my_macro.sas replaced the old. That process does not need to change. What should change is that a second macro library should be created containing every version of the macro. Within the folder /historical/macro/library, all these files would reside, each holding a different definition of %MY_MACRO:

- my_macro.20121124, holding the original version of the macro.
- my_macro.20130308, holding the first revised version.
- my_macro.20130703, holding the second revised version.
- my_macro.20131015, holding the third revised version.

The last portion of each file name matches the first day that the macro was in effect, replacing the previous version of the macro. With these pieces in place, two pieces of information would be sufficient to determine which version of the macro should run:

- The name of the macro (in this case, my_macro).
- The date. Based on the files named above, a date of 20130805 would imply that the most recent version was from 20130703.

A macro call might define which version of which macro(s) should be in effect:

```
%backdate (macro_list=my_macro,
          as_of_date=20130805,
          folder=/historical/macro/library)
```

The intent would be that all calls to %MY_MACRO use the variation that was in effect as of August 5, 2013. The %BACKDATE macro could take these steps:

1. Inspect the historical macro library. Retrieve a list of all file names that define %MY_MACRO.
2. Compare the dates in the file extensions to the user-specified &AS_OF_DATE.
3. Select the extension that is closest to, but less than or equal to, &AS_OF_DATE. Provide an appropriate error message if &AS_OF_DATE precedes all the available file extensions.

4. %INCLUDE the selected file, defining %MY_MACRO.

SAS can accomplish all of these steps, with a little help from the operating system.

13.2 The Steps

Step 1: Retrieve a List of File Names in the Folder

Each operating system uses different tools to accomplish this task. Under UNIX, for example, this command would work:

```
ls /historical/macro/library/*.* > some_file.txt
```

The pieces of this command work as described below:

```
ls
```

This command requests a list of all file names:

```
/historical/macro/library/*.*
```

This is the folder and name pattern to search for. *.* indicates any two-part name with a dot separating the parts:

```
>
```

This symbol indicates that the list of names should be directed to a given location rather than displayed:

```
some_file.txt
```

This is the destination file that will hold the list of names.

Once this command has executed, some_file.txt will contain the full list of file names, such as:

```
/historical/macro/library/my_macro.20121124
/historical/macro/library/my_macro.20130308
/historical/macro/library/my_macro.20130703
/historical/macro/library/my_macro.20131215
/historical/macro/library/your_macro.20130102
/historical/macro/library/your_macro.20130414
```

Each operating system will have its own methods for extracting a list of file names. The remainder of this section will demonstrate just the UNIX example that begins with the steps illustrated thus far.

The next task is to convert the UNIX command to a form that a SAS program can run. The X command allows SAS to run an operating system command. This macro serves as a starting point:

```
%macro backdate (macro_list=,
                 as_of_date=,
                 folder=/historical/macro/library);

    x "ls /historical/macro/library/*.* > some_file.txt";

%mend backdate;
```

Within the X command, both the input folder and the output file should have some flexibility. Choosing the input folder is easy enough:

```
    x "ls &folder/*.* > some_file.txt";
```

But naming the output file requires a little more work. Wouldn't it be nice if macro language handled this for you? For example, suppose this program called %BACKDATE:

```
/my/program/folder/prog1.sas
```

Automatically, macro language could create this file, holding the list of file names:

```
/my/program/folder/prog1.macro_list
```

While not illustrated here, it would be wise to add a fourth parameter to the macro that permits the user to designate the name of the output file. If that parameter is left blank, the macro would use the logic below to supply the name. Before diving into that logic, however, let's briefly examine some of the issues. What benefits accrue by having the program determine the name of the output file?

This approach provides many advantages:

- The list of macro names would always be stored in a known location.
- That list could serve as documentation at a later date, showing which macros were actually available within the historical macro library.
- The programmer would not be burdened with having to name the output file.
- Multiple programs running at the same time would never contend for the same output file.

There would be disadvantages as well:

- Because the output file name depends on the program name, %BACKDATE could not run in interactive mode (unless a fourth parameter were added).
- The programming becomes more complex if %BACKDATE runs multiple times in the same program (particularly if there might be more than one historical macro library involved). These complications lie beyond the scope of this chapter.

Section 4.2 showed how to create an output file that matches the program name. This statement would retrieve the full program name:

```
%let prog_name = %sysfunc(getoption(sysin));
```

Assuming the program name always ends with .sas, the statements in **bold** could be added to the macro:

```
%macro backdate (macro_list=,
                 as_of_date=,
                 folder=/historical/macro/library);

   %local output_file;
   %let output_file = %sysfunc(getoption(sysin));
   %let output_file = %substr(&output_file,1,%length(&output_file)-3);
   %let output_file = &output_file.macro_list;
   x "ls &folder/*.* > &output_file";

%mend backdate;
```

Notice that the middle %LET statement removes "sas" from the end of the name, but it does not remove the dot before that. Therefore, the third %LET statement requires just one dot, not two.

Step 2: Convert the List of Macros to a SAS Data Set

Having retrieved a list of all file names, the macro must convert that list to a SAS data set. The plan is to use that SAS data set to determine which file holds the properly dated version of %MY_MACRO. Here is one approach to preparing the SAS data set:

```
data all_macros;
   infile "&output_file" lrecl=200 pad;
   length filename    $ 200
          macro_name  $  32
          filedate    $   8;
   input filename $200.;
   filedate = scan(filename, -1, ".");
   macro_name = upcase(scan(filename, -2, "./"));
run;
proc sort data=all_macros;
   by macro_name descending filedate;
run;
```

The INPUT statement must apply an informat. Some folder names may contain a blank, rendering list input insufficient.

Values for FILENAME will typically take this form:

```
/historical/macro/library/macroname.YYYYMMDD
```

The SCAN function uses delimiters of . and / to select:

- FILEDATE holds YYYYMMDD. The -1 word is the first word when reading from right to left.
- MACRO_NAME holds the name of the macro. The -2 word is the second word when reading from right to left.

Step 3: Find the Proper Macro Definition

For each macro that the user includes in &MACRO_LIST, the program must:

- Identify the files that could potentially define the right macro.
- Compare FILEDATE to &AS_OF_DATE.
- %INCLUDE the proper file.

Even with a large macro library, the data set of macro definitions might contain on the order of 10,000 observations -- small enough to process multiple times. The idea is to process the list within ALL_MACROS for each macro that must be defined. This code would locate the proper definition of %MY_MACRO:

```
data _null_;
   set all_macros end=nomore;
   where macro_name = "MY_MACRO";
   if filedate <= "&as_of_date" then do;
      call execute("%include '" || trim(filename) || "';");
      stop;
   end;
   if nomore;
   put "ER"
       "ROR:  The macro MY_MACRO could not be located."
     / "as_of_date=&as_of_date, folder=&folder";
   call execute("endsas;");
run;
```

Because the file names are sorted by both MACRO_NAME and descending FILEDATE, the first matching file will be the correct one. "Matching" means that the name of the macro is correct, and the date is on or before the user-specified &AS_OF_DATE.

When the matching file is located, the program should %INCLUDE it and then halt the DATA step. CALL EXECUTE (followed by the STOP statement) handles these tasks. And if no matching file exists, the user should receive a message about that before halting the program.

In order to define multiple macros with a single call to %BACKDATE, loop through the same process for each macro in the list:

```
%local i next_macro_name;
%if %length(&macro_list) > 0 %then
%do i=1 %to %sysfunc(countw(&macro_list, %str( )));
    %let next_macro_name = %upcase(%scan(&macro_list, &i, %str( )));
    data _null_;
        set all_macros end=nomore;
        where macro_name = "&next_macro_name";
        if filedate <= "&as_of_date" then do;
            call execute("%include '" || trim(filename) || "';");
            stop;
        end;
        if nomore;
        put "ER"
            "ROR:  The macro &next_macro_name could not be located.";
        put "as_of_date=&as_of_date, folder=&folder";
    run;
%end;
```

Each iteration through the %DO loop defines one macro from &MACRO_LIST.

13.3 The Implementation

All of the code from Section 13.2 gets incorporated into the final definition of %BACKDATE. After you have added the optional fourth parameter, the complete macro definition becomes:

```
%macro backdate (macro_list=,
                 as_of_date=,
                 folder=/historical/macro/library,
                 output_file=);

%local i next_macro_name;
%if %length(&output_file)=0 %then %do;
    %let output_file = %sysfunc(getoption(sysin));
    %let output_file = %substr(&output_file,1,&i-3);
    %let output_file = &output_file.macro_list;
%end;
x "ls &folder/*.* > &output_file";

data all_macros;
    infile "&output_file" lrecl=200 pad;
    length filename    $ 200
           macro_name  $  32
           filedate    $   8;
```

```
        input filename $200.;
        filedate = scan(filename, -1, ".");
        macro_name = upcase(scan(filename, -2, "./"));
    run;
    proc sort data=all_macros;
        by macro_name descending filedate;
    run;

    %if %length(&macro_list) > 0 %then
    %do i=1 %to %sysfunc(countw(&macro_list, %str( )));
        %let macro_name = %upcase(%scan(&macro_list, &i, %str( )));
        data _null_;
            set all_macros end=nomore;
            where macro_name = "&macro_name";
            if filedate <= "&as_of_date" then do;
                call execute("%include '" || trim(filename) || "';");
                stop;
            end;
            if nomore;
            put "ER"
                "ROR:  The macro &next_macro_name did not exist as of";
            put "&as_of_date, folder=&folder";
        run;
    %end;

%mend backdate;
```

This application requires an output file that holds a list of all files in the historical macro library. Therefore, the first %DO group checks whether the user specified the name for an output file. If not, the program computes the name as program_name.macro_list. In practice, the user will often leave &OUTPUT_FILE blank and allow the program to compute the name.

Next, the program reads that output file, producing a SAS data set holding one observation for each file in the historical macro library. A sample observation might look like this:

FILENAME: `/historical/macro/library/my_macro.20130308`

MACRO_NAME: `MY_MACRO`

FILEDATE: `20130308`

With the data sorted by MACRO_NAME DESCENDING FILEDATE, the program is ready to locate the proper definition of each name in &MACRO_LIST. Each iteration through the final %DO loop defines one macro, performing these steps:

1. Find the name of the next macro in &MACRO_LIST.
2. Read in the SAS data set holding the name of every file in the historical macro library.
3. Process those file names that match the name of the next macro in &MACRO_LIST.

4. When the names match, compare the dates. Because the incoming file names are in sorted order from latest to earliest date, the first observation falling on or before the &AS_OF_DATE is the right one.
5. Use CALL EXECUTE to generate a %INCLUDE statement for the proper file. The %INCLUDE statement executes automatically when the DATA step finishes.

Is it magic? Perhaps it seems that way. But once you practice the tricks and techniques, your macros will perform magic as well.

13.3.1 Programming Challenge

The final programming challenge doesn't appear in a book. It will arise in many forms, as you program and as you field requests from end users. Can you assimilate what you have learned and utilize appropriate techniques? Can your attitude be, "I'll find a way to make that happen"? Can you apply tools in new, innovative ways to expand upon what you have seen here?

I wish you the very best as you rise to the occasion.

Index

CPSIA information can be obtained at www.ICGtesting.com
Printed in the USA
LVOW11s1747140913

352426LV00003B/11/P